COLLINS GEM

CARD GAMES 2

The Diagram Group

D0932879

HarperCollinsPublishers

HarperCollins Publishers
P. O. Box, Glasgow G4 0NB

A Diagram Book first created by Diagram Visual
Information Limited of 195 Kentish Town Road,
London NW5 8SY, England

First published 1992
© Diagram Visual Information Limited 1992
Reprint 10 9 8 7 6 5 4 3 2 1

ISBN 0 00 470123 2

Printed in Great Britain by
HarperCollins Manufacturing, Glasgow

Introduction

Collins Gem Card Games 2 brings together more than 80 games and variations that are played for stakes. Some are games of chance, some of skill; most involve an element of both.

The book is divided into four sections for easy reference. Social Games are those played among friends and at parties. Poker – the most popular competitive card game in the world – is given its own section because of its many variations, from Anaconda to Spit in the Ocean. The games in the Family Games section are not always played competitively, but are described here with rules for playing at home for small stakes. Banking Games – such as the widespread Blackjack – are those that are usually played in casinos and clubs, where players gamble against the banker. *Collins Gem Card Games 2* offers something for everyone. Some games are suitable only for older players; others can be played by any age-group. Each game is described with step-by-step instructions, complemented by clear, explanatory diagrams. In addition, tips on strategy and surefire techniques – as well as the extensive glossary of terms used in competitive card playing – will turn even the novice player into an expert!

Created by the Diagram Group, this book is the perfect companion volume to the same team's *Collins Gem Family and Party Games* and *Collins Gem Card Games*.

Contents

SECTION 3. FAMILY GAMES

SECTION 4. BANKING GAMES

Glossary

ACTIVE PLAYER One who is still in the game and has not dropped out or been eliminated.

ANTE To put up a stake or place a bet before the cards are dealt.

CHIPS Counters used for placing stakes or bets. In gambling games, chips have a monetary value.

COINS Small denominations are often used in social and family games instead of chips.

COURT CARDS The K, Q and J of each suit.

CUT Dividing a deck of cards into two parts after a shuffle and reversing their positions. The dealer is often determined by cut. Each player cuts the deck and reveals the top card. Depending on the game, the player with the highest card (high cut) or lowest card (low cut) deals. There must be at least five cards in a cut.

DEAD CARD or DEADWOOD Cards not used in melds (as in Gin Rummy) or in hands (as in Poker).

DEAL The way cards are distributed among players at the start of a game.

DECK Playing cards used for a particular game. The standard deck is 52 cards, i.e. four suits of thirteen cards each.

DEUCE The 2 of each suit.

DISCARD To throw a card away. Also used to describe the card thrown away and the pile onto which it is thrown.

EXPOSED CARD Same as UPCARD.

FOLLOW SUIT Playing a card of the same suit as the previous one.

GO KNOCKING Unable to play a card.

HAND A name given both to the cards dealt and the play using those cards.

HOLE CARD A card on the table which is unknown to everyone.

LEADER The player to the left of the dealer, who conventionally leads by playing the first card in most card games.

LEADING SUIT The suit of the first card played.

MELD A group of cards of the same rank, as opposed to a SEQUENCE. To meld means to lay out a meld or add one or more cards onto an existing one.

ODD CARD A single, unpaired card.

ODDS Chances of winning. Odds of 2 to 1 against, when playing with a bank, mean that out of every three tries, the bank has two chances and the player one chance of winning.

PACKET A group of two or more cards dealt together.

PASS When a player does not play or bid.

POKER HAND Hand of five cards on which players win or lose according to the rank of their hands. There are ten standard hands and two more when wild cards are in use.

POOL Same as POT.

POT The central collection of stakes. Can literally be a pot to hold chips or coins. Sometimes called the pool.

RAISE Bet in Poker when a player stakes the same amount as a previous player plus an extra amount. Players usually say 'raise you two' or whatever the amount by which the bet is being raised.

RANK Order of cards or suits in play. Higher ranks take precedence over lower ranks.

SEQUENCE A run of cards of the same suit.

SHOWDOWN When everyone shows their hands.

SHUFFLE To mix the cards, by hand. In private games every player has the right to shuffle the cards, but the dealer must make the final shuffle before the deal. In club games only the house dealer shuffles.

STAKE The number of chips that are being bet.

STAND PAT Remaining in play but not drawing a card. Sometimes simply called 'stand' or 'stick'.

STOCK Cards remaining after the deal from which additional cards are drawn during the game.

STRIPPING Removing certain cards from a standard deck of 52 cards.

SUIT Clubs, spades, hearts and diamonds.

TRICK A group of cards, one from each player in turn according to the rules of the game.

TRUMP A suit that outranks all others, which are called plain suits.

UPCARD A card that is turned up, from the deal or the stock, to start a discard pile or to designate trumps. Sometimes called the exposed card.

WIDOW An extra hand dealt to the centre of the table. It usually remains unexposed unless the game allows a player to exchange his or her hand for it.

WILD A card that can be used to replace any other card. Usually the joker is a wild card.

About competitive card games

Card games form a spectrum, with games almost entirely dependent on skill at one end, and games entirely dependent on chance at the other; most fall somewhere in between. All such types are represented in this book.

All the games in this book are 'competitive' in that they are played for stakes – whether chips or coins – that are bet on players' forecasts of the outcome of the game. Winning depends on careful forecasting as well as careful play – and, of course, on luck.

Raffles, lotteries and tombolas are pursuits based on chance. Guessing at the number of peas in a jar or the position of a ball in a photograph of a football game, while still based a great deal on chance, do to some extent require skill. In these activities, however, the odds are long – i.e. heavily stacked against the participants.

In the competitive card games in this book, in contrast, the odds are short and fair, which adds to the pleasure of playing them. After all, they are *games*, to be won or lost but always enjoyed.

TYPES OF COMPETITION
Competing by forecasting performance

In many of the games, individuals or partners try to forecast their performance from the hand of cards they have been dealt.

The forecast, or bid, is often backed up by declaring a
stake, which can make the game more exciting.

Competing with a stake

Stakes may be placed by using counters, chips,
matchsticks or very small coins. These are won or lost
according to whether a forecast or score has been
achieved or not.

Games can also be played for stakes without making a
forecast.

Competing for a high score

In this kind of game, players often cannot forecast the
outcome because they are dealt very few cards. They
have to make the best possible use of whatever cards
come up, while remembering which cards have been
disposed of on a throwaway pile. Players compete to
make the highest possible score.

Competing for the pool

In some of these card games, there is an extra challenge
to skill and wit if all the players place an equal stake in
a central pool before play commences. The pool is then
won by the player who gets the highest score for the
round, or for the whole game. For example, one counter
from each of four players at the beginning of a round
makes a pool of four counters.

Competing for a cumulative pool

In some games the pool, or pot, can only be won at the
end of a round if a player has achieved an agreed score.
If nobody gets that score for the round, the pool
remains and everyone places another counter in the pot,
thus increasing its value.

The competitive element can be stimulated further by
agreeing forfeits for certain situations. For example,

when playing incorrectly or making a misdeal, a player may be required to pay another counter into the pool.

The size of a stake

If it is decided to use stakes, it is useful for everyone to begin with the same number of counters. Twenty counters each would be enough for most games. A series of games can be declared finished when one player has lost all his or her counters. Then a new session can begin by sharing out the counters equally again.

Easy Go

This is a game of pure luck which offers everyone an equal chance of winning. It is an excellent game to illustrate the unpredictability of luck. Even in the fairest situation, a person can win or lose several games in succession before his or her luck changes. Given enough games, probably several thousand, everyone would win and lose an equal number of times.

Players

Up to nine can play. Easy Go is a game of chance between players and the dealer, sometimes called the banker. Players take on the role of banker in turn.

Cards and chips

One standard deck of 52 cards is used, aces ranking high. Each player needs about 40 chips.

Dealing

The first dealer is the person who cuts the highest ranking card from the pack. Thereafter, the deal goes to the next player clockwise.

The dealer gives one card face up on the table to each player, beginning on the left.

Playing

The dealer places the next card face up on the table. Each player who has a card of the same rank, but the opposite colour, as this card must pay one chip into the pot. Those having a card of the same rank and the same colour pay two chips into the pot.

The dealer places another four face-up cards, one at a time on top of the first card. At each turn, the players pay progressively larger numbers of chips.

Number of chips to be paid into the pot

Card	Same rank, opposite colour	Same rank, same colour
first	1	2
second	2	3
third	4	5
fourth	8	9
fifth	16	17

A sample first deal and payments due to the pot

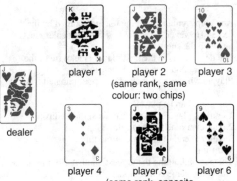

player 1

player 2
(same rank, same
colour: two chips)

player 3

dealer

player 4

player 5
(same rank, opposite
colour: one chip)

player 6

After the payout on the fifth card, everyone is dealt another card. The dealer again turns the first of five cards face up on the table.

This time, for every card of the same rank, each player takes chips OUT OF the pot in the same amounts.

Number of chips to be taken from the pot

Card	Same rank, opposite colour	Same rank, same colour
first	1	2
second	2	3
third	4	5
fourth	8	9
fifth	16	17

Any chips remaining in the pot are claimed by the dealer. However, if the pot is short, the dealer must make up the shortfall.

The deal passes to the next player clockwise of the dealer for another round of the game.

Players who lose all their chips are eliminated from play.

The game can be played:

1 until all players but one have lost their chips;

2 until everyone has had a deal;

3 until the end of an agreed time limit.

Winning

The person holding the highest number of chips at the end of the game is the winner.

Ecarté

Originating in 18th-century France, Ecarté is a fast-moving game for two players. The name of the game means 'discarded'.

Competition

Players aim to be the first to score 5 points. Use of a pool is optional.

Cards

All cards below 7 are stripped from a standard 52-card deck to make a deck of 32. The rank from high to low is K, Q, J, ace, 10, 9, 8, 7. Two cards make a trick.

Rank

high   low

Aim

The aim is to score points by making tricks.

Preparing

Paper and pencil are needed for keeping the scores. Using the ranking of the 32-card deck, players cut for first deal and choice of deal for the whole game.

Dealing

The first dealer shuffles the cards and invites the non-dealer to cut. The dealer then deals five cards face

down to the opponent and five to him- or herself, in
packets of three then two or in packets of two then
three.

The eleventh card is placed face up on the table to
determine trumps. If it is the K, the dealer gains 1 point.
The remaining cards are piled face down to form a
stock. If either player holds the K of trumps, and
chooses to declare it, he or she gains a point.

The deal

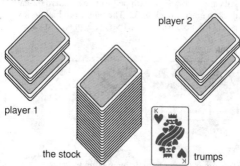

player 2

player 1

the stock

trumps

The exchange

An exchange of cards can take place before play
commences but only if the non-dealer proposes one and
the dealer accepts.

To exchange, the non-dealer discards cards face down,
which are then dead. This player is then dealt the same
number of replacement cards face down.

The dealer can then make exchanges. This process continues until stopped by the dealer declaring 'play' or until the stock pile runs out. At this point play must start.

An exchange cannot be proposed by the dealer but he or she can continue to exchange after the non-dealer calls 'I play'.

An exchange should not be proposed or accepted if a player holds cards with which at least three tricks could be made.

Playing

The non-dealer leads with one card face up. The dealer must play a card of the same suit if possible. If not, the next option is a trump card; failing both, the dealer can play any other card.

Tricks are won by the card of the leading suit that is higher in rank or by a trump card.

If trumps are led, only a higher ranking trump wins the trick.

The one winning a trick leads the next, and so on until all five tricks are complete.

Scoring

There are four ways of gaining points.

a Three tricks gain 1 point.

b Five tricks, called a vole, gain 2 points.

c K of trumps gains 1 point (see **Dealing**).

d Two points are gained if an opponent fails to make three tricks after standing or refusing an exchange.

Winning the game

A player who has 5 points wins.

Five Hundred Rummy

One of the Rummy family, this game is sometimes
called Pinochle Rummy and is one of the oldest
versions still popular for competitive play with chips.

Cards and players

The game can be played by two to eight players. With
two to four players, one standard deck of 52 cards is
used. For more players, two standard decks will be
necessary.

The most exciting game is said to be when there are
three or four players.

Ranking of cards and their points value

The ace can be low or high, but runs cannot 'go round the
corner' i.e. one cannot have a run of, for example, Q, K,
A, 2, 3. The court cards count as 10 points each, the ace
counts as 15 points when ranked high and 1 point when
ranked low, and all other cards count at their face value.

Dealing

Players cut the cards for the deal; the lowest cutter deals.
He or she deals thirteen cards each if there are two
players, seven each if there are more than two players.
The remaining cards are placed face down on the table
to form the stock and the top card is turned face up to
start the discard pile.

Aim

As with all Rummy games, the aim is to make melds
(three or four cards of the same rank) and sequences or
runs (three or more cards of the same suit in sequential
order). In Five Hundred Rummy, the aim is to make the
highest score from these melds and sequences.

Sample values of melds and sequences

meld of three 9s (value: 27 points)

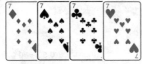

meld of four 7s (value: 28 points)

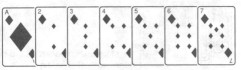

sequence of ace to 7 (value: 28 points)

sequence of Q to ace (value: 35 points)

Playing

Beginning with the player on the dealer's left, each
player, in turn, takes a card and throws one away on the
discard.

As the cards are thrown onto the discard, they are
spread out so that everyone can see the position of each
card in the pile.

the discard spread out

the stock is also spread out to
guard against cheating

The card a player takes may be from:
1 the top of the stock;
2 the top of the discard;
3 lower down the discard, in which case all the cards
above it must also be taken.

If a player chooses option 3, the desired card must be
used immediately to lay down a meld or a sequence.

The card thrown away may be either from the hand or

the stock card just picked up. A discard picked up may
not be thrown away at the same turn.

Between taking and throwing away, a player may lay
down on the table any melds or sequences made.

Cards may also be laid onto the melds or sequences of
other players, in which case the player must declare
this. Players keep these cards in front of them, not with
the meld or sequence onto which they are laid, to make
scoring easier.

Ending the game

The hand may end in one of two ways.

Ending one. The game ends when one player melds all
his or her cards. The losers then count the points value
of all cards they each still hold in their hands and
deduct that total from the total value of cards they have
each already laid on the table.

The resulting score for the game may be positive or
negative.

Ending two. Another way the game ends is when the

Sample game scores

(chip value: 20 points)

Player	Score	Deduct from 502	Chips to pay
1	234	268	13
2	21	481	24
3	170	332	6
4	502	winner	

Total: 53

The winner gains 13 + 24 + 16 = 53 chips.

stock is exhausted and the player whose turn it is cannot meld any more cards. At this point, some players allow everyone to lay down any cards they can on melds and runs anywhere on the table.

The points are then counted as before.

Winning the game

The first player to reach a positive score of 500 or more points wins the game. That player then collects chips from each player equal to the value of the difference between their two scores (see table).

Strategy

In this game it is crucial to lay down as many cards as possible and not hold them in the hand any longer than necessary.

Gin Rummy

This skilful, cut-throat game was first known as Gin Poker. It became known as Gin Rummy because of its similarity to Rummy. The game has developed much since being invented in 1909, and enjoyed a surge in popularity in 1939 when it was taken up by the Hollywood crowd. As a result, variations of rules are played in different locations. For the purposes of this book, we have used the standard rules as defined by John Scarne, the great card-game expert, in his many books.

Players

Only two play at a time. If there are more people wishing to play they can do so in rotation, but only two at a time.

Competition

Each player aims to win chips by having a score that is considerably lower than the opponent's. The greater the difference in scores, the greater the winnings.

Cards

A standard deck of 52 cards is used in which ace ranks low. The cards count at their face value, ace being worth 1 point and court cards 10 points each.

Rank

high   low

Point values

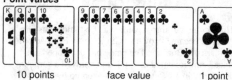

10 points   face value   1 point

Preparing

To keep the game moving quickly it is best to use two
decks of cards with different patterns on the back.
The decks are used alternately. While one deck is in
use, a non-player can shuffle the other deck in readiness
for play in the next hand.
If there are only two players, both decks are shuffled at
the same time, and one deck is put aside ready for
immediate play in the next hand.
Paper and pencil will be needed to record the scores.
Chips may also be used if desired. All players should
begin with the same number of chips; 20 each would be
sufficient.

Points value of the chips

This should be agreed before the game begins. Players
new to the game should first compete for points. Once
familiar with scoring systems, a points value of chips
can be decided.

Aim

Players try to make melds (three or four cards of the
same rank) or sequences (a run of three or more cards
of the same suit).

Dealing

The two players decide who shall shuffle the cards.

**A sample meld and sequence
made from a ten-card hand**

meld of four Js

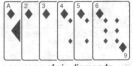

sequence of six diamonds
from ace to 6

Both players then cut the pack. The one cutting the
lowest ranking card is the first dealer. The other player
will be the next dealer.

The dealer then shuffles the cards. The opponent may
also shuffle them if desired but the dealer has the right
to make the final shuffle.

The dealer asks the opponent to cut the shuffled cards.
If the offer is refused, the dealer cuts them. When
cutting cards there must be at least five cards in either
section.

If two decks are being used, the opponent should
shuffle the second set at the same time.

The dealer begins with the opponent and deals one card
to each of them alternately, until they both have ten
cards.

The dealer turns up the 21st card and leaves it face up
on the table next to the remaining stock, which is
placed face down.

The stock should be spread out a little to prevent two
cards being picked up from it by mistake.

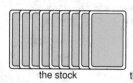

| second deck set aside | the stock | the upcard |

The upcard

The first card turned up onto what will become the discard pile is called the upcard.

The points value of the upcard should be recorded on the score sheet to avoid dispute later, because it determines the maximum number of points a player may have left in hand if that player decides to go out by knocking.

For example, if the upcard is valued at 5 points, the total points value of the unmatched cards in the hand of a player who knocks may not be more than 5.

The unmatched cards are known as the deadwood and their total points value is the deadwood count.

When the upcard is an ace, a player may not knock and has to go gin, i.e. has to make melds or sequences of all the cards in the hand.

Playing

The non-dealer starts by either taking the upcard or refusing it.

If refused, the upcard can be taken by the dealer.

If the dealer doesn't take it, the non-dealer must then take the top card from the stock.

Whoever takes a card, whether upcard or top of the

Sample hand of a player knocking

meld of three 4s plus a run of hearts

deadwood count is 3

upcard value is 5

Sample hands of players going gin

a run of ten diamonds

melds of four aces and three 6s plus a run of three clubs from 6 to 8

stock, must then throw one card from his or her hand face up onto the discard pile.

Each player continues in turn to choose to take either the top of the discard or the top of the stock, and to throw away one card, which may not be the card just picked up from the discard but can be the one picked up from the stock.

Play continues until one player decides to go out.

the stock   the discard

Going out

There are two ways of going out: by going gin or by knocking. Either can only be declared after picking up and discarding a card in turn.

1 Going gin. When able to make melds and/or sequences with all cards in hand, a player places the discard face down on the table and calls 'gin', laying down his or her cards face up in their appropriate sets. The opponent must then lay down all his or her cards face up, sorting them into any melds or sequences already collected and totalling the deadwood count. The deadwood count is credited to the winner, who also gets a bonus of 25 points for going gin.

2 Knocking. When a player decides to knock because

Sample hands when one goes gin

Winner's hand

discard   gin hand of two melds and a sequence

Loser's hand

a meld and a run   deadwood count of 28

the deadwood count in hand is less than the value of the first upcard, he or she plays the discard face down and calls 'knocking'. That player then lays down the other cards in hand, face up in sets, including the deadwood cards, and announces the deadwood count.

The opponent than lays his or her cards face up on the table and may discard in the following ways:

a by making melds or sequences of three or more cards;

b by adding any suitable cards to the knocker's melds;

c by setting aside cards to the same points value as the knocker's deadwood count.

The opponent then counts his or her remaining unmatched cards. This is the score for the hand, known as the box. It is credited to the knocker's score.

Sample hands when a player knocks
Knocker's hand

discard   one meld and one sequence   deadwood counts 5

Opponent's hand

one meld and one sequence   deadwood counts 32

Score for the hand, credited to the knocker,
is 32 − 5 = 27

Underknocking
If the opponent's deadwood count is lower than or
equal to that of the knocker, this is called
underknocking. The opponent then wins the box plus a
bonus of 25 points plus the difference in points total
between the two hands.
If the deadwood counts are the same, the opponent wins
the hand by scoring a bonus of 25 points.

Sample hands in an underknock

Knocker's hand

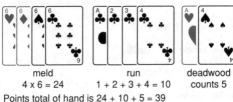

meld	run	deadwood
4 × 6 = 24	1 + 2 + 3 + 4 = 10	counts 5

Points total of hand is 24 + 10 + 5 = 39

Opponent's hand

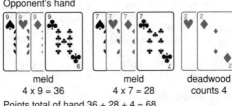

meld	meld	deadwood
4 × 9 = 36	4 × 7 = 28	counts 4

Points total of hand 36 + 28 + 4 = 68

The opponent wins the hand because his or her deadwood count is lower than the knocker's. The opponent's score is therefore:

box score	=	1
bonus score	=	25
difference	=	29 (i.e. 68 – 39)
TOTAL SCORE	=	55

Declaring no game

When there are only two cards remaining in the stock,

Sample scoring

(D = dealer; ND = non-dealer)

	Score/running total	
Hand	**D**	**ND**
1 D knocks 7. ND has 22.		
D scores 22–7=15.	15/15	—/—
2 ND knocks 3. D has 29.		
ND scores 29–3=26.	—/15	26/26
3 D goes gin. ND has 18.		
D scores 18+25 gin bonus.	43/58	—/26
4 ND knocks 4. D also has 4.		
D gets 25 underknock bonus.	25/83	—/26
5 ND goes gin. D has 15.		
ND scores 15+25 gin bonus.	—/83	40/66
6 D goes gin. ND has 46.		
D scores 46+25 gin bonus.	71/154	—/66

Dealer has reached a score of over 150, so the game ends and bonuses are added to the scores.

Final scores for the game	154	66
Box bonuses		
D won four boxes of 25 points	100	
ND won two boxes of 25 points		50
Game bonus goes to D	150	
TOTAL SCORES	404	116
Deduct loser's score from winner	116	
Winner's final score for the game	288	

the next player may pick up the discard and knock or go gin, but may not pick up from the stock. If that player cannot go out either way, the hand is declared a no game and a new hand is dealt.

Scoring

The game ends when a player scores 150 points or more. Bonus points are then added to each player's totals as follows:

1 each player gets 25 points for each box won during the game; and

2 the winner of the game gets a bonus of 150 points. The loser's total for the game is then deducted from the winner's score. The result is the final game score that goes to the winner.

Winning the competition

Chips are paid by the loser to the winner, according to their value – for example, one chip per point or one chip for every 10 points.

A new game can then be started. If there are more than two players, the winner then plays with a new opponent.

If the game is being played for chips, scores are not carried forward to the next game so both players begin with a clean score sheet.

If chips are not being used, players carry forward winning scores from one game to the next.

The payout

The loser pays the winner. If one chip is worth 1 point, the loser (in the sample) pays 288 chips. If one chip is worth 10 points, 28 chips are payed. If coins are being used, then if one penny is worth 1 point, the loser pays £2.88, and if one penny is worth 10 points, 28p is paid.

Hearts and Variations

Hearts used to be called Reverse because the aim is to avoid winning points. The game is excellent for competitive play with or without chips. The variations add interesting options to the basic game, which is known as Pure Hearts.

PURE HEARTS

This is a game of skill for three to six players, playing for themselves.

Cards

A standard 52-card deck is used with ace ranking high.

Rank

high   low

Certain cards are stripped from the deck, according to the number of players, as follows:

three players: remove one black deuce;
four players: no cards removed;
five players: remove both black deuces;
six players: remove one black 3 and all deuces except the 2 of hearts.

Competition with chips

Each player puts the same stake into a central pot. The winner of the game will take the pot.

Before dealing, it should be agreed how much the stake shall be.

Aim

The aim is to make tricks but avoid taking tricks containing any hearts cards. A trick is a collection of cards, one from each player in turn, played face up on the table.

Sample tricks when there are three players

second player
could not follow suit so discarded
the 2 of spades

Dealing

Players cut for the deal. Anyone has the right to shuffle the cards but the dealer makes the final shuffle and cut. All the cards are dealt out equally to all players, beginning with the player to the left of the dealer. There is no trump card and no bidding for how many tricks can be made.

During a game, the dealing passes in turn clockwise.

Playing

Beginning with the player on the dealer's left, each

person plays one card face up. Players must follow the leading suit. If a player cannot follow suit, then any other card may be played, including hearts.

The player of the highest card of the leading suit takes the trick and leads the next trick with any card in hand.

The game ends when all cards have been played.

Scoring

Tricks have no points value, but each hearts card counts as 1 point against the player. However, if a player takes all thirteen hearts cards during the hand, no penalty points are counted. This tactic may be tried by a player who has been dealt a large number of hearts and thinks it possible to draw out the rest in tricks won.

Winning

Skilled players will keep careful count of which cards have been played and of where cards are likely to be distributed. They will also be adept at visualizing possible moves.

The winner of the pot is the player with the lowest score at the end of a game. Playing hearts for chips can be expensive for the unskilled.

The winner of the game becomes the dealer for the next one.

AUCTION HEARTS

This variation of Pure Hearts requires the strategic use of chips for bidding before play begins.

As in Pure Hearts, the aim is to make tricks but avoid those made in what is called the minus suit, which may or may not be hearts.

The minus suit is declared by the player who makes the highest stake.

Bidding

After the deal, made as in Pure Hearts, players view their hands carefully and decide which of the four suits they would like to call as the minus suit. They should also consider how important it is that their bid should succeed.

Beginning with the player on the left of the dealer, each player bids for the right to call the minus suit by placing chips in the pot.

Players can bid any amount or pass. The bid can be raised on the next round of bidding, by adding the extra amount to the pot.

The player who makes the highest bid wins the right to call the minus suit and to lead play.

Playing

Play proceeds as in Pure Hearts, with players trying to avoid taking any tricks that contain minus suit cards.

Strategy

Bidding should never be done recklessly. The best situations in which to make a bid are when a player holds either no cards in a certain suit or only one card in a suit with low numbers in other suits.

If a player wins a bid for the minus suit and has one card in that suit, it is best to lead play with that card.

It is also wise to bid defensively when holding many cards in one suit, in order to prevent someone else declaring it the minus suit.

Scoring and settling

Any player with minus suit cards in tricks at the end of the hand is 'painted'.

A point is counted against painted players for every minus suit card they have taken in tricks collected during the hand. A chip is paid into the pot for every point. Any player with no minus suit cards in tricks at the end of a hand is 'clear'. A clear player collects the pot. If there are two clear players, the pot is shared, and odd chips are carried over to the next pot.

If one player has taken all thirteen minus suit cards, leaving three clear players, the pot then becomes a jack and is carried over.

The jackpot

When nobody has won the pot, it is carried over to the new deal for the next hand as the jackpot and no bidding takes place. The original highest bidder declares the minus suit.

Only when there is a winner of the previous hand does bidding take place in the next hand.

BLACK LADY

This is a variation based on the special place given to the Q of spades as a penalty card. This game is also known as Black Maria, Calamity Jane or Slippery Anne.

Playing

Black Lady is played in the same way as Pure Hearts, but the Q of spades carries 13 points which, like all

Point values

all heart cards score 1   Q of spades scores 13
penalty point each   penalty points

other points, count against the player who has the card at the end of the hand.

Versions of Black Lady

All versions are played the same as Pure Hearts.

Version 1. The player holding the Q of spades tries to play it on a trick that will be won by someone else, loading the 13 points onto the one who takes the trick.

Sample tricks with four players

player of ace of spades takes the trick and the 13 points

player of Q of clubs takes the trick and the 13 points

Version 2. The player holding the Q of spades can only play it on a trick in which he or she cannot follow suit. The Q should then be played on the first such trick.

Some tricks containing the Q of spades

player of ace of diamonds takes the trick and the 13 points

player of K of hearts takes the trick and the 13 points

player of 4 of diamonds takes the trick and the 13 points

Version 3. The 'pass' takes place before play begins. Players view their own cards and choose three to pass face down to the player on their left, who must take them. When there are five or more players, only two cards are passed.

Players should beware of passing high spade cards other than the Q. They can be used, with some lower ranking cards, to control the suit.

Only high-ranking hearts cards should be passed; it is good strategy to pass a club or diamond if holding several.

Scoring and settling

Settling is exactly as for Pure Hearts, counting the Q of spades as 13 points.

PINK LADY

This is played in the same way as Black Lady, with the Q of hearts counting as 13 points as well as the Q of spades. The game ends when one player reaches a score of 100 points.

CANCELLATION

This variation is for six to ten players using two standard 52-card decks, which are shuffled together as one pack.

All the cards are dealt until everyone has the same number. The remaining cards form the widow. The player taking the first trick also takes the widow in hand.

The rule of cancellation

This variation is played as in Black Lady except that when identical cards are played on the same trick, they cancel each other out.

Cancelled cards are not used to take the trick. If all the cards in a trick are cancelled, which can happen when there is an even number of players, the trick is given to the player who takes the next trick.

A completely cancelled trick made by six players

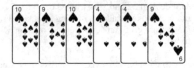

Scoring and winning

The two Qs of spades each count as 13 points; all other cards count as 1. When one player reaches a score of 100, the player with the lowest score wins the game and takes the pot.

DRAW HEARTS

This is a variation of Pure Hearts for two players.

Both players are dealt thirteen cards and the remaining cards form a stock, face down on the table.

At each turn, both players draw an extra card from the top of the stock; the player winning the trick draws first and the loser draws second.

When the stock is exhausted, the game continues to its conclusion as in Pure Hearts.

Hoggenheimer

Also known as English Roulette, this is a competitive
game played between a banker and any number of
players.

Cards and chips

A standard deck of 52 cards is stripped of all the 2s, 3s,
4s, 5s and 6s. A joker is added, making a deck of 33
cards. Players are given an equal number of chips with
which to bet.

Aim

Players try to win chips by making successful bets on
cards that will be exposed before the banker turns up
the joker.

The banker

Participants bid for the position as banker. The highest
bidder is the banker and deals the cards.

The banker pays out and collects on the bets made by
the players.

The player on the left of the banker takes over the
position when certain conditions are completed in play
(see **Change of banker**).

Dealing

Any player has the right to shuffle the cards, but the
banker makes the final shuffle.

The banker deals the cards face down on the table in
four rows of eight cards. The odd card is left face down
at one side for the moment.

Each row in the layout is given the name of a suit in the
following order, top to bottom: spades, hearts,
diamonds, clubs. The columns, left to right, represent
the rank order of the cards, from ace down to 7.

Example of the layout with stakes in place

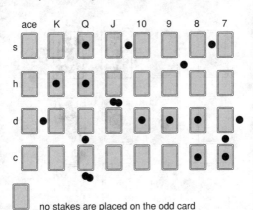

no stakes are placed on the odd card

More than one player can place the same bet.

Placing bets

All players, except the banker, place bets by putting chips on any cards they reckon will turn up before the joker is exposed.

Players can make bets of any size, in any order, on as many cards as they like.

A player may want to bet that two neighbouring cards will both turn up before the joker, in which case the stake is placed between the cards.

Losing the bank as the last club is turned

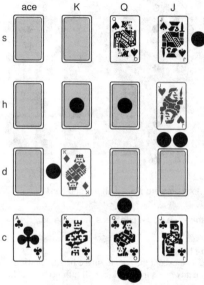

stakes remain in place as the game continues

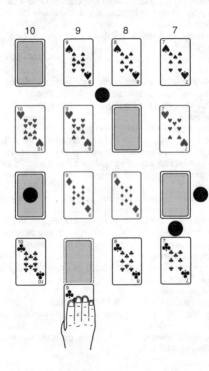

A stake is placed at the adjoining corners of four cards if a player wants to bet that all four cards will turn up before the joker.

Similarly, a player can bet that a whole suit will be turned up before the joker. In this case the stake is placed at the right-hand end of the appropriate row of cards.

To bet on all four cards of the same rank, the player places the stake below the appropriate column.

When the betting is complete, the banker proceeds.

The odds

When a bet is won, the banker pays:

a evens on one card, i.e. the same amount as the stake;
b 2 to 1, i.e. twice the stake, on two adjoining cards;
c 4 to 1 on four adjoining cards or all of one rank; and
d 8 to 1 on a whole suit of eight cards.

Playing

The banker turns the odd card face up. If it is the joker, the deal ends and the banker wins all the stakes. If it is another card, the banker puts it in its correct position in the layout, removing the card that is already there and paying out on any stakes placed on it, according to the odds given above.

The removed card is then placed into its proper position in the layout, the card there is removed, and the bet is paid out as before.

This replacement of cards continues until the joker appears. When that happens, the banker claims all remaining stakes.

The banker then shuffles the cards, deals the layout and invites new bets.

Change of banker

The banker loses the bank when a complete suit of cards is turned up before the joker. The new banker is the player to the left of the banker.

Alternative rules allow for a change of banker when either four aces or four 7s appear.

A player whose turn it is to be the banker may choose to auction off the position to the highest bidder before play begins again.

Winning the game

The game can continue for an agreed length of time or number of deals, as long as all players have chips. The player with the most chips, or the last player with chips, wins the game.

Variation

Instead of using chips, players can make their bets with coins, giving a monetary value to the winnings. The banker then pays out bets on the odds as usual, but the value of each bet is determined by the value of the coin used. For example, a player winning a 20p bet on four adjoining cards turning up before the joker wins odds of 4 to 1, and so is paid 80p.

Kalooki

Also known as Caloochi, Kaluki and Kalougi, this
game is similar to Rummy, with some additional
interesting rules.

Players

A game for two to six players, it calls for the most skill
when played by four, each person playing individually.

Competition

Kalooki can be played for points, for chips or for both.
If chips are to be used, players should begin with an
equal number and drop out if all their chips are used up.
A reasonable starting number of chips would be 60
each. Players should agree the number of chips before
the game begins.

If chips are to have a monetary value, each player
should buy chips by placing coins into a pot before the
game begins. In this case, a player who has lost all his
or her chips may be allowed to buy more, adding their
value in coins to the pot.

Cards

Two standard 52-card decks and four jokers are needed.
Ace can rank high or low and can be part of a sequence
that runs 'round the corner', i.e. K, ace, 2.

The cards carry points values as follows:

ace:	11
court cards:	10
other cards:	face value
jokers:	wild. A joker has the same value as the card it represents; unplayed it counts as 25 points.

Cards

two decks   four jokers

In a meld of three or four jokers, each joker counts as
15 points. However, they are usually more useful as
wild cards.

Dealing

The first dealer is chosen by drawing from the pack.
Cards are dealt clockwise beginning from the dealer's
left. Each player is dealt fifteen cards if there are two to
four players. If there are five players, the deal is
thirteen cards each; for six players, eleven cards each.
The remaining cards are placed face down in a pile to
form the stock.

Aim

Players try to get rid of all their cards by making melds
or sequences.

A meld is three or four cards of the same rank. A
sequence is three or more cards of the same suit in rank
order.

Playing

The player to the left of the dealer begins by taking one
card from the top of the stock and discarding one from
his or her hand.

Some examples

melds

sequences

The discard may be the card just picked up from the stock. It is placed face up to begin a discard pile next to the stock.

Play continues clockwise in turn, each person taking a card and discarding one.

Each player tries to build a first meld with a value of at least 51 points. When one player has achieved this, the meld is laid down on the table, face up, at that player's turn.

A player may not take the top card from the discard pile unless it can be used in that player's first meld.

Melds and sequences are laid down after taking a card and before making a discard.

A sequence of 54 points

$$7 + 8 + 9 + 10 + 10 + 10 = 54$$

Advantages after the first meld or sequence

Having made a meld or sequence, players have three privileges:

1 they have the choice of taking a stock card or a discard;

2 at their turns, players can lay off any cards on the melds of other players; and

3 subsequent melds can be of any points value.

Ending the game

The game is finished when a player goes out by laying out the last of his or her cards.

A player who goes out may dispose of one card on the discard, but is not obliged to do so.

If a player goes out by laying down all cards at once (which must include a meld valued at 51 points or more) he or she makes a Kalooki.

Scoring

Players are credited with the points value of the cards they have laid out on the table during the game.

The losers also count the points value of cards remaining in their hands at the end of play. These totals are then added to the winner's score.

It is usual to play as many games as there are players, so each person takes a turn both at dealing and leading play.

The overall winner is the player with the highest final score.

Settling

If it has been agreed to play with chips, settling is done at the end of each game.

The losers pay the winner one chip for every card they were left holding at the end of the game and two chips for every joker.

If the winner makes a Kalooki, the losers pay double.

When all the games have been played, players cash in their chips by taking their value in coins from the pot.

Knock Rummy

This is a fast version of Rummy and the forerunner of Gin Rummy.

Players

The game is played by any number from two to five.

Competition

Players compete for points and may also win chips from each other on the strength of their scores.

If chips are used, everyone begins with an agreed number, the amount depending on which method is used (see **Winning chips**).

Method one. Twenty chips each would be sufficient.

Method two. Players would need about 500 chips each. Players who lose all their chips drop out.

Play can continue until there remains one final winner, who holds all the chips, or until an agreed time limit is reached, when the overall winner is the one holding the largest number of chips.

Cards

A standard deck of 52 cards is used; ace ranks low. Cards count at face value, with court cards worth 10 points and aces 1 point.

Value of cards

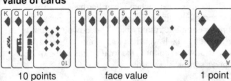

10 points   face value   1 point

Dealing

Players cut the cards for the first deal. Thereafter the deal passes to the winner of the hand.

Beginning with the player on the left of the dealer and continuing clockwise, each player is dealt one card face down, then a second card on the next round and so on. For two players, the deal is ten cards each. For three or four players, the deal is seven cards each. When five play, the deal is six cards each.

The remaining cards are placed face down to form the stock; the top card is then turned over to start the discard pile.

Aim

Players aim to make sufficient melds (three or four cards of the same rank) and sequences (a run of three or more cards of the same suit) to win the hand by knocking.

Playing

As in basic Rummy, each player takes a card from the stock or the discard, and throws away a card, which may not be the card drawn from the discard.

Melds and sequences are held in the hand and only laid on the table when a player knocks to end play.

Knocking

To knock, a player picks up a card, knocks on the table and discards a card when his or her hand is either:

1 a complete rummy (all melds and sequences); or

2 not a complete rummy but the deadwood count is estimated to be lower than that of any other player.

The deadwood count is the total points value of a player's unmelded cards.

Strategy

Defensive play, i.e. discarding high-value cards to
avoid heavy losses, is often the best strategy.

Good observation of the discards is essential for
judging the best moment to knock.

Some players follow certain established notions of what
the deadwood count should be to knock successfully.
For example, between two players it is safe for one
player to knock on a deadwood count of up to 60 on the
first turn, 40 on the second, 30 on the third and so on by
10 points per round. Between three players, the first
round deadwood count should be less than 35, and
between more than three players, less than 30. On
subsequent rounds the count should be 20, 15 and then
less than 10.

Rigid adherence to in this system, however, often leads
to disaster, because other players are skilfully adapting
their strategy as they observe the discards.

The break

When the number of cards remaining in the stock is
equal to or less than the number of players, nobody
may knock.

When the stock equals the number of players, the
player who picks up the next stock card is the breaker
and must lay on the table all completed sets of melds
and sequences but keep the other cards hidden in hand.
Players in turn then each take a stock card and lay
down all completed sets from their hands. Instead of a
stock card, a player may take the discard if it can be
immediately added to an existing set. Players can also
lay off cards on the sets laid down by previous players.

When the stock is used up, each player in turn then lays down the remaining deadwood cards, declaring their points value. The player whose deadwood has the lowest count is the winner.

In the case of a tie, the player who was the breaker wins. If the breaker did not tie, the tied player nearest to the breaker's left wins.

Scoring

When someone knocks, play stops and each player counts the points value of only the deadwood cards, first showing all melds and sequences before discarding them.

If the knocker's deadwood count is less than that of any other player, the knocker wins.

If the knocker has gone rummy and has no remaining deadwood, the knocker wins outright.

If the knocker fails to win the hand, the player with the lowest deadwood count wins.

The knocker remains the winner if another player's score ties with that of the knocker's.

Winning chips

Method one (according to John Scarne)

1 The successful knocker is paid one chip each by all the other players.

2 The unsuccessful knocker, who loses because another player has fewer points, pays this player, known as the underknocker, two chips. All the other players pay the underknocker one chip each.

3 If a player has gone rummy, i.e. laid down all cards, each of the other players pay that player three chips.

4 If a player goes rummy by laying down all cards in a sequence of the same suit, then each player pays that player six chips.

Method two (according to Carl Sifakis, another card game authority)

1 The successful knocker is paid, in chips, the difference between the other players' deadwood count and the knocker's deadwood count.

2 The unsuccessful knocker pays each player as many chips as the difference between that player's deadwood count and the lowest deadwood count.

3 If the knocker has gone rummy by melding all cards in a sequence of the same suit, the knocker is paid a bonus of 25 points by each player.

Loo

Once one of the most popular and widely played
European card games, Loo and its many variations are
played for stakes.

THREE-CARD LOO

This variation is for three or more players; six players
make the game most interesting.

Competition

Players compete to win the pool or part of it.

Cards

A standard 52-card deck is used. Ace ranks high.

Aim

Each player attempts to win at least one trick. Failing to
take a trick, known as being 'looed', scores a penalty.
Players should agree beforehand whether to play
'limited Loo' or 'unlimited Loo' (see **Looing**).

Dealing

Players cut for the deal. The lowest cutter shuffles and
deals three cards, one at a time and face down, to each
player. An extra hand, called a 'miss', is also dealt,
either as the first or the last hand of a round. The next
card is dealt face up to indicate the trump suit; the
remainder of the cards form the stock.

The pool

Players each put three counters into the pool. The
dealer may choose to make the opening deal a 'single'
by not dealing a miss. Then only the dealer puts three
counters into the pool. Only the opening dealer has the
option to deal a single.
The deal passes clockwise in subsequent deals.

The choice

Starting with the player on the left of the dealer, each player chooses one of the following:

a to play with the cards in hand, saying 'I play';

b to throw in the hand and take the miss, saying 'I take the miss'; or

c to pass, saying 'I pass' while throwing in the cards, taking no further part in that deal.

If everyone passes, the dealer takes the pool.

If only one player has chosen to play and has taken the miss, the dealer has the option of either playing or letting that player take the pool.

If only one player chooses to play but has not taken the miss, the dealer must play using the cards in the miss. In that case, whether having won or lost, the dealer neither gains nor loses counters.

Playing

The player who first chose to play then leads with the highest trump, if holding one. Each player who did not pass follows suit in turn, trying to take the trick with a higher card. If a player cannot follow suit, any other card may be played, preferably a trump to take the trick. As a last resort a player may discard.

The player winning the trick must lead with a trump whenever possible.

Scoring

Each player who wins a trick takes one-third of the pool.

Looing

Any player who does not take a trick is said to be 'looed'. If limited Loo is being played, looed players pay a penalty of an agreed number of counters (usually three) into the pool. If unlimited Loo is being played, the looed player must pay a penalty of as many counters as there were in the pool at the start of the hand.

Penalties

Players are also looed for:

a playing out of turn;

b looking at the miss but not taking it; and

c not leading with the ace of trumps when able to.

Variations of the rules

1 The trump suit is only revealed when a player cannot follow suit.

2 If three trumps are dealt to one player, the player collects the pool, the hands are thrown in and shuffled, and a new deal is made.

FIVE-CARD LOO

Another variation, this game is played as for Three-card Loo with the following differences.

Dealing

Five cards are dealt to each player. A miss is not dealt.

Pool

Five rather than three counters are contributed.

Exchanges

Players may choose to exchange cards from their hands for up to five cards from the stock, but must then play their new hands.

Pam

The J of clubs is called 'pam'. It outranks all other cards, regardless of which suit is trumps. When leading with the ace of trumps, a player may say 'pam be civil', which means that pam cannot be played to that trick.

Flushes

A flush is five cards of the same suit, or four cards plus

pam. A player who holds a flush shows it before play
and wins the pot. All other players are then looed
unless they also hold a flush or a flush with pam.
A five-trump flush wins the hand and the pot. In a tie of
two equal flushes, the one with the highest ranking card
wins. In a tie of two or more plain-suit flushes, the pot
is divided equally.

Sample flushes

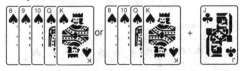

pam

Blazes

A hand made of only court cards is a blaze; it outranks
a flush. A player who is dealt a blaze wins the hand and
the pot. In a tie of two blazes, the one with the highest
ranking card wins.

Sample blazes

pam

Napoleon

Also known as Nap and similar to Contract Bridge,
Napoleon is a game for two to six people, each playing
individually. A game of four players makes the best
opportunity for skilled competitive play.

Cards

A standard deck of 52 cards is used in which ace ranks
high.

Rank of cards

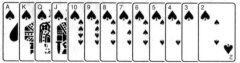

high   low

Competition

Players compete to win chips and to avoid losing them.
Each player will need to begin with at least 200 chips.
Since gains and losses can be quite dramatic, it is
recommended that only experienced players credit
chips with a financial value.

Making tricks

A trick consists of one card from each player in turn.
The person playing the highest ranking card of the
leading suit wins the trick, unless it is trumped.
The trump suit outranks all other suits. A trump card

can be used to trump and take any trick, providing the player cannot follow the leading suit.

Sample tricks made by four players

no trumps   hearts are trumps

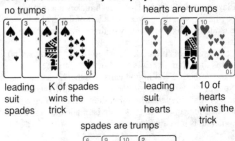

leading   K of spades   leading   10 of
suit   wins the   suit   hearts
spades   trick   hearts   wins the
                                          trick

spades are trumps

leading suit   2 of spades
diamonds   wins the trick

Aim

Each player tries to make tricks and prevent the highest bidder from fulfilling his or her contract.

The highest bidder tries to collect chips by making the number of tricks bid. Players who fail to make their bids pay out according to the number of tricks they bid.

Dealing

The players cut for the deal. Subsequent deals rotate clockwise.

Each player is dealt five cards. The remaining cards are put aside, face down; they are not needed until the next deal.

Bidding

Players study their cards and each makes one bid, beginning with the player to the left of the dealer.

Each person bids to make two, three, four, five or no tricks.

The first bid of five tricks is called 'nap'. A player who wants to outbid nap calls 'wellington', and one who wants to outbid wellington calls 'blücher'.

Note that when wellington or blücher is bid, there are two or three players who think they can each make five tricks. Since only five tricks can be made altogether, someone is miscalculating.

Bidding

A bid to make no tricks, i.e. to lose every trick, is called 'misère' or 'null' and ranks between three and four tricks.

If the bidding is won with a bid of misère, the hand is played without trumps.

The player who makes the highest bid is known as the bidder for that hand.

Rank order of bids

A bid higher up the list outbids one lower down.

Bid	Number of tricks
blücher	5
wellington	5
nap	5
four	4
misère	0 (played with no trumps)
three	3
two	2

Playing

The bidder leads with one card, the suit of which becomes trumps for that hand.

Each player must follow suit, adding one card. If a player cannot follow suit, any other card may be played. This first trick is won by whoever plays the highest trump card.

The winner leads to the next trick and players must follow suit. Anyone who cannot follow may play any other card, including a trump card.

The trick is won by whoever plays the highest ranking card in the leading suit, if no trumps are played.

If one or more trump cards have been played, the
highest trump card takes the trick.

Play continues until all five tricks have been made.

Settling

There is no scoring in Napoleon. If the bidder wins, he
or she collects from each player. If the bidder loses, he
or she pays each player.

The most usual system for settling is according to the
payout table below.

The payout

Tricks bid	Bidder wins and collects from each player	Bidder loses and pays to each player
two	2 chips	2 chips
three	3 chips	3 chips
four	4 chips	4 chips
nap	10 per trick = 50	5 per trick = 25
wellington	10 per trick = 50	10 per trick = 50
blücher	10 per trick = 50	20 per trick = 100
misère/null	15 chips	3 chips per trick made

VARIATIONS

Purchase Nap

In this variation, after the deal the remaining cards are
placed face down to make a stock.

Instead of bidding, players may, in turn, exchange any
card in the hand for an unseen card from the top of the
stock on payment of one chip to a central pot.

Players may only make an exchange five times. Play
then begins, with each player attempting to make a nap,
i.e. take all five tricks.

Hands are dealt and played until a player makes a nap and wins the pot.

If there are several deals and exchanges before a player makes a nap, the pot can be substantial by the time it is won.

Seven-card Nap

In this version each player is dealt seven cards, and the highest bid is for seven tricks. Wellington and blücher are not used.

The payoff collected for a winning bid of six tricks is 18 chips per trick, and for a winning bid of seven tricks is 24 chips per trick.

If the bidder loses, the payoff is halved.

Newmarket

This British version of the game is also known as
Michigan, Saratoga, Chicago and Boodle.

Players

Newmarket is a game for three to eight players, each of
whom begins with ten chips.

Competition

Players can compete for either chips or coins. Chips can
be given a monetary value by being 'bought' from a
central pool. The value of chips should be agreed
before playing.

Each player begins by buying ten chips from the pool.
The money for these purchases remains in the pool
until the end of play.

A player who loses all ten chips can buy more from the
pool in groups of ten.

Cards

A standard 52-card deck is needed plus four extra cards
from another pack.

These four should be an ace, K, Q and J, each from a
different suit. They are known as the boodle cards and
are laid out face up on the table, where they remain
throughout the game.

Players place their bets on the boodle cards.

Laying out the stakes

Before the cards are dealt, each player places all ten
chips on the boodle cards in any way he or she likes:
some on each boodle card; a few on one card and the
rest on another; or all on one card.

Rank order

high  low

boodle of different suits

Sample stakes for a game with five players
boodle cards

Aim

Players try to acquire chips by:

a playing one or more of the boodle cards and claiming the chips on it; and

b winning the hand by being first to get rid of all their cards, in which case all other players pay the winner.

Dealing

Players cut for the deal, the highest cutter dealing.

All 52 cards are dealt, beginning with the player on the dealer's left and ending with an extra hand to the dealer's left, called the widow.

The cards are dealt singly, face down. When the deal is complete, some hands may have an extra card, depending on the number of players.

The widow hand remains face down on the table.

The deal when there are three players

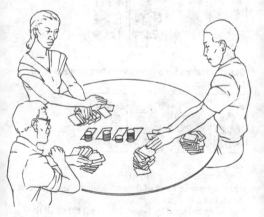

There are thirteen cards in each of the four hands.

The widow

In Newmarket, the widow hand usually remains dead and nobody knows what it contains.

In other versions of the game, the widow belongs to the dealer, who may exchange his or her own hand for it without knowing what it contains. The dealer's hand then becomes the widow, which remains dead.

If the dealer doesn't want the widow, it can be auctioned off to the highest bidder. The bidder's hand then becomes the widow and remains dead.

If nobody wants the widow it is left untouched.

Playing

The player to the dealer's left opens by playing, face up, the lowest ranking card in hand. If that player holds any cards of the same suit to follow it in rank order sequence, those are played as well.

Whoever holds the next card in sequence plays it. Players add cards to the sequence until the run is completed with the ace or is stuck because the next card is in the widow.

The person on the left of the last player then plays the lowest ranking card in hand, which can be in the same suit or in another suit.

Whoever plays one of the boodle cards collects the chips staked on that card.

End of a game

The game ends when one person has played all his or her cards. The winner then collects from each player one chip for every card each is left holding.

Strategy

Basic Newmarket is very much a game of chance with only limited opportunity for strategic play, because

An example of cards in play

Players may agree to let cards remain in view, as here, or prefer that cards are closed up, so that those played earlier cannot be seen.

nobody knows which cards are in the widow.

If the widow is available for exchange, as in the Michigan version of the game, at least one person will know what the dead cards are because they were previously in that player's hand, which was exchanged by right (as the dealer) or by auction. This player has ample opportunity to use this knowledge strategically. Careful observers will also note how eagerly the dealer claims the widow. If there is a lot of competition during the bidding for the widow, it is likely that several players hold no boodle cards.

A hand with no boodle cards should not necessarily be exchanged. If there are several high-ranking cards, there is a good chance that the player can be first to play out.

The next game

The boodle cards always remain on the table. If any of the stakes have not been claimed, they are left on the boodle. Chips are then added, as before, in readiness for the next game.

In some versions of Newmarket, any remaining stakes are played for by shuffling the cards and dealing them all out face up. Whoever is dealt a boodle card claims anything on it. This method is useful at the end of an evening's play. However, during play, it is more interesting to let unclaimed boodle chips accumulate from one game to the next.

The winner of a game becomes the dealer for the next game.

The Spin variation

Spin or Spinado is not a game in its own right but a variation of several games.

In Spin Newmarket, or Spin Michigan, the ace of diamonds is wild and can be used in place of any card. It adds extra spice to an already exciting game.

It is very useful, for example, when a player has the card next in sequence below a boodle card. Then the wild card can be played to collect the boodle chips.

If the ace of diamonds is to be used as a wild card, the ace in the boodle should be of a suit other than diamonds.

Polignac

An old French party game that is played for chips.
Polignac is also known as Four Jacks or Quatre Valets.

Competition

Each player pays into a central pot to purchase an equal
number of chips.

For social purposes, ten chips worth a small coin would
be adequate.

For more serious play, the value of the chips should be
agreed before play begins; more than ten can be
purchased, providing everyone has the same number.

Players

Polignac is suitable for four to six players. The deck of
cards varies with the number of players and the type of
game.

Cards

A complete standard deck of 52 cards is used if the
game is to be social. Ace ranks high. The Js of clubs,
hearts and diamonds each carry 1 penalty point. The J
of spades is known as the 'polignac' and carries 2
penalty points.

If players of equal skill (or lack of it) wish to play for
serious stakes, the pack is stripped according to the
number of players.

For four players, all cards below the rank of 7 are
stripped to leave a deck of 32 cards.

For five or six players, the deck is also stripped of both
black 7s, leaving 30 cards, which, when dealt, will give
an equal number to each player.

Rank and penalty points

high   low

1 penalty point   polignac
                                   2 penalty points

Playing with the stripped decks requires a good memory.

Aim

The players make tricks and try to avoid taking any of the Js, which carry penalty points.

Dealing

After players have bought their chips, they cut for the deal. Anyone may shuffle the cards but the dealer has the final shuffle and invites the player on the left to cut the cards.

Beginning with the player on the dealer's left, all cards are dealt. Each player has an equal number of cards.

Stripped deck for five or six players
high   low

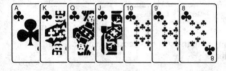

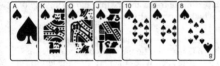

Tricks

A trick is a collection of cards, one from each player in turn. The player who leads determines the leading suit which must be followed, if possible, by all other players.

A player who cannot follow suit may play any other card.

There are no trump cards, so only the highest ranking card in the leading suit can take the trick.

Sample tricks – social play

four players

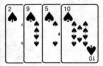

10 of spades takes the trick

five players

ace of hearts takes the trick

Sample tricks – serious play
four players

ace of diamonds takes the trick

Only the Q, J, 10 and 8 of diamonds remain to be
played, so much skill lies in leading tricks correctly.

five players

K of spades takes the trick and 2 penalty points from
the polignac (J of spades)

Only the ace and 9 of spades remain to be played.

Playing

The player to the left of the dealer leads to the first trick.

Tricks are taken by the person who plays the highest ranking card in the leading suit.

The winner of the trick leads to the next trick.

When the hand has been played, a reckoning is kept of who has the penalty points: 1 for J of clubs, hearts or diamonds and 2 for the polignac.

Players who have penalty points pay one chip per point back into the pool.

The cards are shuffled and dealt by whoever took the final trick in the last hand.

Winning the game

Hands are played until one player has lost 10 points, i.e. all ten chips in the social game. When that happens, the player who has the lowest number of points, i.e. the highest number of chips remaining, takes the pot.

To start another game, players then purchase enough chips from the pool to bring their total back to 10, paying the value of the chips into the pot.

Pope Joan

A very old game, Pope Joan is a combination of the
earlier games Commit and Matrimony. It was once
extremely popular in Scotland among religious
reformers.

Players

Any number can play, but three to six players are best.

Cards

A standard 52-card deck is stripped of the 8 of
diamonds, leaving a deck of 51 cards. Ace ranks low.
The 9 of diamonds is known as the pope or Pope Joan.
In the days of the Scottish Reformation, it was
nicknamed 'the curse of Scotland'.

Rank

high   low

the pope or
Pope Joan

Competition

The game is played for chips or coins; everyone begins
with the same number. Thirty chips per player per game

is a good starting number. Only the dealer lays out chips so, to complete a game, every player must deal once.

The Pope Joan game board

Originally, Pope Joan was played with a circular board divided into eight compartments. Now, eight small containers or saucers can be used instead. Alternatively, keen players may like to make their own board or divide a sheet of paper or card into eight sections. The eight sections are labelled, as was the original board: pope, intrigue, matrimony, J, Q, K, ace, game.

The board

Aim

Everyone tries to take chips from the board by playing certain cards and by being the first to play all their cards in a hand.

Choosing the dealer

Players cut the cards to decide the first dealer. Subsequent deals pass clockwise until everyone has dealt once.

Dressing the board

When the dealer has been chosen, but before the cards are dealt, the dealer 'dresses the board' by placing chips in the sections as shown in the table.

Section	Chips
pope	6
intrigue	2
matrimony	2
J	1
Q	1
K	1
ace	1
game	1

A total of fifteen chips is staked by the dealer.

Dealing

Everyone has the right to shuffle the cards but the dealer makes the final shuffle and invites the player to the left to cut the cards.

Beginning with the player on the dealer's left, all the cards are dealt out.

An extra hand, the widow, is dealt into the centre of the table, before the dealer's own hand.

The widow hand remains face down and is not used in play.

Players must have the same number of cards, so any surplus card goes onto the widow's hand.

The last card dealt is turned face up onto the widow and left exposed.

The exposed card

If the exposed card is the pope, the dealer takes the

chips from the pope section on the board and a new
hand is dealt by the player to the left of the first dealer.
If the exposed card is not the pope, it indicates the
trump suit for that hand – for example, 4 of clubs would
make clubs the trump suit.

If the exposed card is an ace, J, Q or K, the dealer
claims the chips on the appropriate section of the board
before the hand is played.

Playing

The player to the left of the dealer plays any card to
begin a sequence. It is usual to call out the name of the
card being played – for example, '7 of hearts'.

Whoever has the next card of the suit in ascending
order, i.e. the 8 of hearts, plays it.

If the dealer or any other player holds two or more
cards in sequence, they can all be played at one time.
Play continues in the leading suit until a stop is
reached.

A run of hearts stopped by the K

Stop cards

A stop is reached when certain cards are played. All the
Ks are stop cards, because they are the highest ranking
cards of each suit.

The 7 of diamonds is a stop card, because there is no 8
of diamonds in the deck.

Other cards may be stop cards either because the next one is in the widow or has already been used to start a sequence.

The player of a stop card turns over the stopped sequence and starts the next one.

A stopped sequence

| 7 of diamonds is the stop card | cards are turned over and a new sequence begins |

Claiming chips during play

Players can claim chips from the board as they play certain cards, as follows:

a playing K, Q, J or ace of the trump suit wins the chips in those sections of the board;

b the J and Q of trumps, played in sequence, win chips from the intrigue, J and Q sections;

c the Q and K of trumps, played in sequence, win chips from the matrimony, Q and K sections;

d when the pope (9 of diamonds) is used, the player claims the chips from that section whether or not diamonds are trumps.

If any of these cards are not played and kept in the hand, they cannot score.

Ending a hand

The hand ends when one person has played all his or her cards. That player then claims the chips from the game section of the board, and also claims one chip per card from the other players. For example, a player left holding six cards would pay six chips.

A player left holding the pope at the end of a hand does not have to pay the winner anything.

At the end of each hand, unclaimed chips remain where they are. New chips are added to the board by the new dealer, before dealing the next hand.

Winning the game

When everyone has been the dealer once, the game ends. Any remaining chips are claimed by a final deal made by the first dealer.

All the cards are dealt but there is no widow so some players may have unequal numbers.

Chips are always claimed according to the following stipulations:

a whoever receives the ace, J, Q or K of diamonds, or the pope, claims any chips on those sections of the board;

b matrimony chips are shared between the players holding the K and Q of diamonds;

c intrigue chips are shared between those holding the J and Q of diamonds.

The winner is the player who has won the most chips.

Alternative betting

Instead of only the dealer laying out chips, all players can place chips in one of two ways, by agreement:

1 all players place the same number of chips on each section; or

2 all players place four chips on the pope, two each on intrigue and matrimony and one chip on each of the other five sections.

To play this alternative, players will need to begin with more chips, such as fifty each.

Rams

An old German game, Rams is played by three to five players.

Competition

Players can compete for chips or buy chips from a central pool and cash them in, if they win any.

If buying from a pool, a value for the chips should be agreed according to how much players want to stake. Ten chips for 1p is a low stake; 10p a chip lifts the stake much higher. At that value, payout on losing the top bid in one hand of six players would be a minimum of 25 chips, i.e. £2.50.

Cards

A standard 52-card deck is stripped of all cards below the 7s down to the 2s. Ace ranks high, so the deck has 32 cards, eight in each suit.

Rank

high   low

Aim

Players try to win chips by taking as many of the five tricks to be won as they can.

Dealing

The dealer is chosen by a cut of the cards, the highest cutter being the dealer.

If six are playing, the dealer does not have a hand.

Before shuffling and cutting the cards, the dealer antes five chips into the pot, even if not playing with a hand. If playing with a hand, this means the dealer must pay the stake before seeing his or her cards.

Beginning with the player on the left, the dealer gives five cards to each player, and to an extra widow hand, in packets of two then three or three then two. The widow remains face down on the table.

The next card is turned up and left on the table. It denotes trumps for the hand.

Any remaining cards are put aside, face down.

Exchanging and bidding to play

Players examine their hands. Each player in turn – except the dealer (see **Dealer's choice**) – has the option to exchange his or her hand for the widow, if it has not already been exchanged.

The player on the dealer's left begins by choosing one of four options:

1 to place his or her hand face down calling 'pass';
2 to exchange the hand for the widow and call 'play';
3 to retain the hand and call 'play'; or
4 to retain the hand and call 'General Rams', which is a bid to take all five tricks.

When General Rams is not bid

All the other players, in turn, call either pass or play. If playing, they may exchange their cards for the widow if it has not already been exchanged.

When General Rams is bid

Whenever a player bids General Rams, everyone must play, so those who have passed must pick up their cards again.

The exchange of the widow proceeds as normal.

Sample bidding

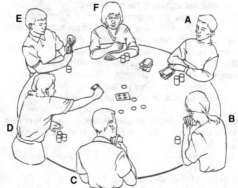

A has bid to pass and will not play unless someone calls General Rams.

B has bid to play.

C has bid to play.

D is about to exchange her cards for the widow and bid to play.

E has not yet made his bid.

F is the dealer and has no cards.

Dealer's choice

The dealer does not bid. If playing with a hand, the dealer can exchange the exposed trump card for one in hand, which is left on the table face up. This action does not change the trump suit.

Obligations

If all players have bid to pass, the last player before the dealer must either play or pay the dealer five chips. (Unless, of course, the player is going to bid General Rams.)

When there is only one player, the dealer must play in opposition.

Playing without a bid of General Rams

After the bidding, the first player who bid to play leads by putting one card face up on the table. All other players must follow suit in turn.

If a player cannot follow suit, then a trump card may be played or a card of any suit discarded.

Taking the trick

The player who played the highest ranking card of the leading suit, or the highest trump card, takes the trick. That player also takes one-fifth of the chips in the pot and leads to the next trick.

Play proceeds in the same way, with each winner of a trick taking a fifth of the pot.

A player who bid to play yet does not make a trick pays a forfeit of five chips into the pot for the following game.

Playing with a bid of General Rams

All players play against the General Rams bidder, who leads to the first trick.

Play proceeds as before, but the General Rams bidder

cannot claim any chips from the pot until winning all
five tricks.

If the General Rams bidder has won all five tricks, he
or she collects the pot and five chips from each player.

If the General Rams bidder fails to take all five tricks,
he or she must double the amount already in the pot and
pay each player five chips.

Winning the game

A game is complete when each player has dealt once in
turn. The winner is the player who has the most chips.
To start a new game, players should begin with the
same number of chips again, cashing in any extra they
have made.

Ranter Go Round

Thought to be an old Cornish game, Ranter Go Round can be played by large numbers and has a children's version called Cuckoo.

Cards

A standard deck of 52 cards is used, in which ace ranks low.

Rank

high   low

Aim

Players try to avoid being left holding the lowest card of the deal.

Competition

Ranter Go Round is a straight gambling game for any number of players.

Each player begins with three chips, which should be purchased from a central pool.

One chip is paid into the pot every time a player loses.

Players drop out of the game as they lose all three of their chips.

The player left in at the end, still holding at least one chip, is the winner and collects all the chips that have been lost by the other players and paid into the pot.

To start a new game, players then purchase more chips from the pool.

How many chips?

If there are ten players, there will be $9 \times 3 = 27$ chips for the winner to claim from the pot (chips are only paid in by the losing players).

If there are fifteen players, there will be $14 \times 3 = 42$ chips.

The winnings can therefore be substantial, depending on the value of the chips.

Players are only risking losing three chips per game.

However, since there is only one winner of each game, players have a one-in-ten chance of winning if there are ten players and only a one-in-fifteen chance when there are fifteen players.

Dealing

The dealer is chosen by cut. After shuffling the cards, the dealer gives one card to each player, beginning with the player on the left.

Playing

The first player (**A**), on the dealer's left, begins by calling either 'stand' (to keep the card) or 'change' (to exchange it).

A changes her card for that of the player on her left (**B**), who is obliged to give up his card, unless it is a K.

If **A** is passing an ace, 2 or 3, it must be declared as the exchange is made.

A player who holds a K does not have to exchange it, but must show it to cancel the exchange.

Then it is the turn of player **B**.

B may call 'stand' or 'change'. If he has a K he will stand.

If **B** calls 'change' he exchanges cards with the next player on the left (**C**).

Play continues clockwise in this way until it is the dealer's turn.

The dealer may stand or change, but if changing, he or she cuts the pack and takes the top card, replacing it with his or her own.

Revealing the cards

If the dealer gets a K from the exchange, it must be

declared because the dealer is then the loser and must pay one chip to the pot.

Otherwise, all players turn their cards face up. The player holding the lowest ranking card is the loser. The loser pays one chip into the pot. In the case of a tie, each loser pays a chip.

A new hand is then dealt by the player to the left of the first dealer.

Winning the game

As players lose all three chips they drop out of the game.

Finally, one player is left holding at least one chip. This player is the winner and collects all the chips paid into the pot.

Red Dog

Also known as High-card Pool, Red Dog was the
favoured gambling game of reporters and their
associates in the pre-television days when newspapers
were the main source of news.

It is a game of skill for up to ten players.

Cards

A standard deck of 52 cards is used. Ace ranks high.

Rank

high   low

Competition

Players compete to win the contents of the pot.

Everyone antes the pot and adds a stake when it is their
turn, so the total staked is often high.

Large amounts can be won and lost quickly in Red Dog.
Friends getting together to play socially should decide
whether to play with:

1 chips with no monetary value;

2 low-value coins; or

3 chips purchased from a common pool.

The excitement of Red Dog comes from the build-up of
the pot when each player loses a bet, so large numbers
of chips should be in circulation.

Aim

Players try to win the pot by gambling on their chances of holding a card that is higher ranking than – but of the same suit as – the one turned up from the stock.

The ante

Before the deal, everyone antes the pot by the same amount. The ante can be as low as one chip each or as high as is agreeable to all players.

Dealing

Everyone cuts the pack. The player cutting the highest ranking card is the dealer.

Starting with the player on the dealer's left, five cards

A sample hand

Player bets that the hand holds a higher card than the stock card, and in the same suit.

Some sample stock cards

a   b   c   d

If the stock card is **a** or **d** this player would win.
If the stock card is **b** or **c** this player would lose.

are dealt to each player, when there are up to eight
players.

The deal is four cards each for nine or ten players.

Playing

The dealer places the remaining cards face down and
only the dealer turns cards up from this stock.

Players study their cards and, in turn, starting from the
dealer's left, bet that they hold a higher ranking card of
the same suit as the card at the top of the stock.

The first player bets by placing chips on the table. Any
number of chips can be staked, from one to the total
already in the pot.

The dealer turns up the top card of the stock and places
it face up on the table.

If the player wins, the winning card is shown and the
player claims his or her own bet plus the same number
of chips from the pot.

If the player loses, his or her entire hand is shown and
thrown in, and the chips bet are added to the pot.

When everyone has had a turn, including the dealer, a
new deal is made by the next player to the left of the
first dealer.

Winning the pot

Play continues until one player wins the pot, or there
are no chips left in the pot.

Then there is a new ante to replenish the pot.

Ending the game

The game should continue until everyone has been
dealer for the same number of times.

Strategy

Every card played is visible, so players who have a
good memory for cards have the edge on those who

haven't. Later players, especially the dealer, have great advantage over leading players because they see all the cards that have been played.

Remembering what has been played helps players to decide if their hands have a good chance of winning. For example, if holding five court cards, the dealer's chances of winning increase if aces are turned up for earlier players.

A strong hand

Mistakes

If the top card of the stock is exposed by mistake, it is put aside and the next card is turned up.

Once a bet has been made, it cannot be changed. Any bet paid to the pool by mistake must stand. Any bet paid out by mistake must stand if the next top card has been exposed.

Fair play

Cheating is easy if three cheats work together, sending each other signals about which cards they hold. For this reason, players should be warned against joining games with strangers.

VARIATIONS

High or Low Red Dog

Players may bet that they hold either a higher or a lower card than the stock card. In either case their card must be of the same suit as the stock card.

GI Red Dog

During World War II a version called GI Red Dog
developed, which gave the dealer even better chances
than in standard Red Dog.

Everyone is dealt only three cards and the dealer has
three turns before the deal passes to the next player.

To compensate for this advantage, only the dealer antes,
putting any stake into the pot.

Play then proceeds as in traditional Red Dog.

Some players of GI Red Dog say the dealer should have
four cards, giving even more of an advantage.

Burn Card Red Dog

In this variation, at each player's turn the dealer
discards the top card of the stock – 'burns' it – after
showing it to all players. The dealer then turns up the
next top card, which determines whether the player has
won or lost.

Rockaway

An adult game for any number of players, Rockaway is similar to the junior version known as Go Boom.

Cards

Two standard packs of 52 cards are needed, making a deck of 104 cards.

The points value of the cards is important: aces count as 15 points; court cards count as 10; and all others count at face value.

Points value of cards

15 points

10 points (24 court cards in all)

All other cards: face value

Aim

Players attempt to use all their cards. When a player achieves this, all others pay into a pot according to the points value of their hands.

Competition

Players agree upon the number of deals they shall each have to complete one game. The game ends after the last deal. Then the pot is divided equally between all players.

Players can play just for chips or for money, purchasing chips from a central pool.

A starting number of 100 chips each would be reasonable.

Dealing

Players cut for the first deal, which rotates clockwise until each player has dealt the agreed number of times.

Beginning with the player to the dealer's left, each player is dealt seven cards face down.

The next card is placed face up on the table and is known as the widow.

The remaining cards are placed face down and form the stock, which is drawn upon by players when required.

Playing

Play is led by the player to the dealer's left.

The player must cover the widow with a card that is:

a of the same suit;

b of the same rank; or

c an ace.

Any player who cannot or does not want to play a card in hand draws from the top of the stock until getting a card he or she can (or wants) to play. All the cards remain in the player's hand.

A player may wish to keep aces in hand to better control the game later on.

When the stock has run out, a player who cannot play onto the widow must miss a turn.

Any card used to cover the widow becomes the new widow.

Paying into the pot

When a player has discarded all cards in hand, the other players count the points value of the cards they still hold and pay the same number of chips into the pot. A new deal is made by the next player.

Playing on the widow

 the widow

cards that can be played

any ace (there are eight)

any 6 (there are seven)

any heart (there are 25)

Sample payments into the pot

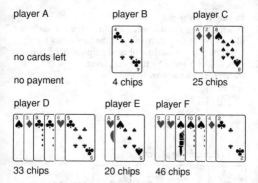

player A

no cards left

no payment

player B

4 chips

player C

25 chips

player D

33 chips

player E

20 chips

player F

46 chips

End of game

When everyone has dealt the agreed number of times,
the pot is divided equally among the players.
Players who have had to pay a lot into the pot recoup
some of their losses. A player who has never managed
to discard an entire hand, but has lost very little each
time, may end winning more than he or she lost.

Slobberhannes

Slobberhannes is popular in Holland and Germany. It is for three to six players. Paper and pencil are needed for scoring.

Cards

All cards below the 7s are stripped from a standard pack of 52, leaving a deck of 32 cards ranking from ace down to 7.

When there are three, five or six players, both black 7s are also stripped from the deck so that everyone is dealt the same number of cards.

Rank

high   low

Competition

There is no betting in this game. All players might lose points during play, but the one who loses the most pays the others in coins or chips.

Aim

Players make tricks but try not to take the first or last one, nor a trick containing the Q of clubs: these tricks all give a penalty point.

Tricks

A trick is one card from each player in turn.

Some sample tricks

three players

ace of diamonds takes the trick

Q of clubs takes the trick
and 1 penalty point

four players

ace of spades takes the trick

J of hearts takes the trick

five players

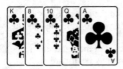

ace of clubs takes the trick and 1 penalty point for the Q of clubs

ace of diamonds takes the trick

six players

K of spades takes the trick

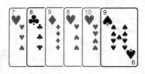

10 of hearts takes the trick

Dealing

The dealer, chosen by cut, deals all the cards starting with the player to the left.

Playing

Players examine their cards and the player to the dealer's left leads by playing any card from the hand to start the first trick.

The next player must play a card of the same suit if possible. If not, any other card may be discarded.

The highest ranking card of the leading suit takes the trick and that player leads to the next trick. There are no trumps in Slobberhannes. Skill is required to discard effectively and to play the Q of clubs without winning the trick.

Ending a hand

The hand ends when all tricks have been made. The deal passes clockwise to the next player, who deals all the cards again, starting with the player on the left. Players keep track of their scores for each hand.

Scoring

Players who take the first or the last trick of a hand, or a trick containing the Q of clubs, lose 1 point for each of these tricks.

If a player takes all three of these tricks in the deal, it is called Slobberhannes. Anyone getting Slobberhannes loses an extra point.

Losing the game

The first player to lose 10 points loses the game and pays all the other players the difference between his or her score and theirs.

Vingt-et-un

Also known as Pontoon, this is a game of chance for any number of players. A version of it is played as the banking game called 21 or Blackjack.

Cards

A standard deck of 52 cards is needed. If there are more than seven players, two decks can be used.

The cards have points values as follows: aces count as 11 or 1; court cards count as 10; all others count at face value.

Individual players may choose to use an ace to count as 11 points or 1 point.

A pontoon

A pontoon consists of two cards that add up to 21. Any ace with any court card or a 10 makes a pontoon.

Pontoons

The bank

The dealer is chosen by cutting the cards; the player cutting the highest card deals.

The dealer is also the banker and everyone plays against the bank.

Everyone then agrees what the maximum stake shall

be. Five chips or small coins, for example, would be a good starting maximum.

Dealing

The banker shuffles the pack and gives each player – including him- or herself – one card face down, starting with the player on the left.

The aim is to collect cards that total 21 points or approach that, but to avoid going over 21.

Playing

Each player looks at his or her own card, replaces it face down and places a stake by it in turn. The stake can be any amount up to the agreed maximum.

Players stake their money (or chips) on getting cards that total 21.

The banker, however, does not place a stake. If the banker has a good card, he or she makes a bet by calling 'double you'.

This means everyone must double the stake already placed by their cards.

A second card is then dealt face down to each player, and they inspect both cards.

If anyone, including the banker, has a pontoon – i.e. an ace and a 10 or a court card – it is revealed and declared.

Payout on a pontoon

1 If it is the banker who has the pontoon, all players pay twice what each has already staked (or four times, if the banker has doubled).

2 If both the banker and another player have a pontoon, that player only 'pays once', i.e. pays the bank the original stake (or twice that stake if the bank has doubled). All other players 'pay twice'.

3 If a player, but not the banker, has a pontoon, the banker pays that player twice the stake (or four times, if the bank has doubled).

4 If two players have pontoons, and the banker has none, the banker pays them both.

Continuing play

If a pontoon has not been made, the hand continues. Before proceeding, however, some players may want to make splits.

Sample splits

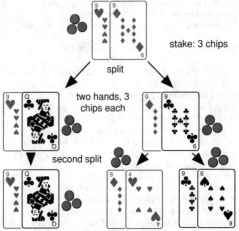

stake: 3 chips

split

two hands, 3 chips each

second split

three hands, 3 chips each

Splits

Anyone who holds two cards of the same rank, such as two 9s or two Js, may split them and have a card dealt on each of them.

If one of the dealt cards is another 9, there could be a further split.

A split must be declared. It is then played as two (or three) separate hands, each carrying the original stake (doubled if the bank has doubled).

Two or more players who want to split in the same round can do so in turn.

If a pontoon is made it must be declared as before.

Play continued: stick, twist or buy

Players now have the option of how their next card is dealt.

The banker begins with the player to the left and asks if players want to 'stick', 'twist' or 'buy'.

If a player's cards add up to 21 or almost 21, the player calls 'stick' (to take no further cards), and the next player takes a turn. Players can only declare 'stick' if the points count of their cards is 16 or more. If the count is 15 or less, players must twist or buy.

'Twist' means a card dealt face up.

'Buy' means a card dealt face down but the player must increase the stake. The amount must not be more than double what is already staked.

If a player buys for an extra stake of, say, two chips, no more than two chips can be staked for any further buys.

A player who has twisted is not allowed to buy on that hand, but may twist on two further turns only.

A player who has bought has the choice of twist or buy again, under the same conditions as before.

Some hands

20 points: stick   25 points: burst   24 points: burst

17 points: stick   19 points: stick

20 points: stick   18 points: stick

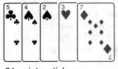

21 points: stick

Five-card, non-bursting hands pay double stakes.

The aim is to acquire cards that add up to but do not exceed 21.

Burst

If a player is dealt a card that takes the total for the hand above 21, the player calls 'burst', throws the cards face up on the table and pays the stake to the bank, taking no further part.

The payout

When everyone has had a turn, the banker puts his or her cards face up on the table and buys or twists cards until either sticking or bursting.

If the banker bursts, each remaining player is paid an amount equal to the player's stake.

If the banker sticks, the remaining players compare the points value of their cards with the banker's. The banker then pays the amount of their stakes to those whose hand has a higher points value than the bank's. Players whose points value is equal to or less than the bank's pay their stakes to the banker.

The five-card trick

The maximum cards a player may collect is five. Any player who collects five cards without bursting is paid double the stake by the bank, regardless of the points value of the cards.

Limitation on buying

A player may buy three cards to make up a five-card trick. However, if the fourth card gives the player a points total of 11 or less, the player is obliged to twist for the fifth card, because it is certain to make 21 or less. A player is not allowed to bet on a certainty.

Changing the bank

A player who gets a pontoon usually takes over the

bank after the deal has been completed, and then shuffles the cards and makes a new deal. There are three conditions under which the deal remains with the same banker:

a when a pontoon is declared in the first round of a new bank;

b when there are two or more pontoons in the same round; or

c when a pontoon has been built on only one of a pair of split cards.

The joker variation

Some players like to include the joker in the pack, which is wild, i.e. it can stand for any card the player chooses.

2. POKER AND VARIATIONS

Poker has been given a separate section because it has so many variations and is the most popular competitive card game throughout the world, especially in the USA. The stakes in Poker can vary from a few coins to thousands of pounds. In the past, many an old prospector and his gold dust were quickly separated by skilled Poker players.

Poker is a simple game. This section begins with the basic rules and is followed by the method of play for some of the more common variations.

About rules

Many rules have been invented in an attempt to guard against cheating. For the purposes of regular games among friends and family members, played in an atmosphere of mutual trust, other rules are best established by agreement over a period of time and written down. This prevents arguments and also enables new friends or colleagues, joining a regularly played game, to read the rules established earlier.

This is probably the best way of learning rules and ensuring that they are kept.

Bluffing versus cheating

The term 'poker face' aptly conveys the art of bluffing at Poker. Players aim to control their facial expressions so that they don't reveal what they are thinking or feeling about their hands in play. The art of bluffing is an indispensable Poker skill.

Cheating, however, is not an accepted part of the game, although there are people who make a profession of it. Hence it is wiser to play with the same group of friends regularly than to join in public games with strangers. Methods of cheating are well documented in dozens of books for those who want to be prepared.

Basic Poker

The procedures explained here are the general rules for all variations of Poker.

Players

The number of players can vary from two to ten.

Competition

Players win by holding the best five-card Poker hand. How the cards are played is often more important than the cards a player holds. Poker is the great game of bluff.

Cards

A standard deck of 52 cards is used, with the occasional addition of one or two jokers as wild cards.

The ace ranks high except when used in any straight to count as 1 in the run.

Rank of cards

high   low

Ace ranks high in a royal flush.

Ace ranks high in an indifferent hand.

This would be called an 'ace-high' hand.

Ace ranks high in tied hands.

In two hands of identical pairs, the one with the higher ranking odd card wins – in this case the hand with the ace. Suits are irrelevant when ranking. This would be called an 'ace-high' hand.

Ace can rank low in a straight flush.

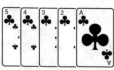

This flush would be a 'five-high' hand because ace ranks low as 1.

Use of two decks

John Scarne, one of the most authoritative voices in the world of card games, suggests that two packs of cards with different back patterns should be used.
Both decks should be thoroughly shuffled. While one is in play, the other is kept at one side to replace it whenever a player makes the request. The change would take place at the end of the current hand.

Seating

Scarne suggests that seating positions at the beginning of a game should be organized as follows:
1 one player is selected by general consensus to shuffle the cards, which are then cut by the player on the right;
2 the shuffler then deals one card face up to everyone, beginning with the player to the left and ending with the shuffler;
3 the person who has the card of highest rank chooses where to sit and becomes the first dealer for the game;
4 the other players then choose their seats, in descending rank order of their cards, from the remaining places.

Changing seats

At the end of an hour of play, any player can ask for a change of seating. The player to the dealer's left then deals for the choice of seats, as before, but also retains the deal for the next hand.

Preparing

Players should agree on the following and write down their agreements on paper:
1 exactly which version of Poker is to be played;
2 which cards, if any, shall be wild cards;

3 a time limit for the game (although everyone has the right to leave the game at any time);

4 who will be the banker and what the value of chips is to be;

5 the maximum and minimum number of chips that can be bet at any one time;

6 a time limit for each play. Five minutes is the usual maximum allowed for a player to decide how to play. Any other active player may call 'time' when the limit is reached, and the hesitant player must drop out. That hand is then dead.

The bank

In a private, social game, players bet with small coins or have a bank and buy chips. In the latter case, one player acts as the banker, and can still take part in the game.

The banker can either be chosen by consensus or by a draw of the cards.

The banker should keep the bank's chips and cash on a separate table.

Before the game starts, the unit value of chips is agreed and players then buy chips from the bank.

At the end of the evening's play, everyone cashes in their chips.

Players can buy further supplies of chips (or can cash some in) during the game. They should do this between hands, while the table is clear.

Coloured chips

Players may decide to use coloured chips, as used in casino games. If they do, then the most common unit values are as follows:

White:	1 unit	Blue:	10 units
Red:	5 units	Yellow:	25 units

Dealing

Anyone can shuffle the cards, but the dealer has the
right to make the final shuffle and offer the cut to the
player on the right.

The cards are then dealt one at a time to each player in
clockwise order. The number of cards dealt to each
player depends on the variation being played.

If there is a misdeal, the dealer collects all the cards,
shuffles and cuts them and deals again.

Aim

Players try to make the best Poker hand possible.

Playing

Beginning with the player on the dealer's left, players
play and bet in turn on their cards, according to the
rules of the particular variation being played.

To bet, each player considers the value of his or her
cards and puts a chosen stake of chips in the central pot.
When the betting is finished and players have their final
hands, there is a showdown.

Winning the showdown

At the showdown, players place their cards face up on
the table.

The player with the best five-card Poker hand takes the
pot. If there is a tie, the pot is shared.

The hands are given a rank order, with those higher up
the list winning over those lower down.

A tie occurs only when the winning hands are identical.
Poker hands rank as shown on the following pages.

Standard Poker hands in descending rank order
1 Royal flush
usually the top-ranking Poker hand (except five of a kind, when using wild cards); the five highest cards in the same suit

An identical royal flush would be the same run in another suit, in which case the two hands tie.

2 Straight flush
a numerical sequence of five cards from the same suit

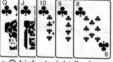

a Q-high straight flush

a 7-high straight flush

a Q-high straight flush

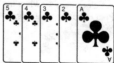

a 5-high straight flush

If two or more players hold straight flushes, the one whose high card ranks over the other's takes precedence.

In these four flushes, the two Q-high hands both outrank the other two and tie with each other for the winning place.

3 Four of a kind
any four cards of the same ranking

The four Ks outrank the four deuces. The odd cards are irrelevant. Two hands of four of a kind cannot tie.

4 Full house
three cards of a kind plus another pair

The hand with the higher ranking three of a kind wins, regardless of the rank of the pair. The full house with three 7s wins over the one with three 6s.

5 Flush
any five cards of the same suit, not in sequence

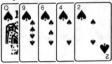

The winner, if there are two flushes, is the hand with the highest ranking card.

If both have the same top-ranking card, the player with the next highest card in rank wins, and so on. If players have identical flushes, there is a tie.

The flush with the K outranks the one with the 10, and wins.

 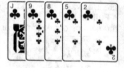

Identical flushes tie.

6 Straight

a run of five cards which are not all of the same suit

The winning straight is the one with the highest ranking card.

The J-high straight wins of these two.

Identical straights tie.

7 Three of a kind
three cards of the same rank and any two odd cards

The winning hand is the one with the highest ranking three of a kind.

Aces rank higher than Js, so the hand with three aces wins. The odd cards are irrelevant. Two hands of three of a kind cannot tie.

8 Two pairs

two pairs of cards plus an odd (unpaired) card

The hand with the highest ranking pair wins.

The ace pair ranks highest.

If two hands have the same highest ranking pairs, the rank of the other pair is taken into account.

The pair of 6s wins over the pair of 4s.

If both pairs match in rank, then the hand with the higher ranking odd card wins.

The 3 ranks higher than the 2.

 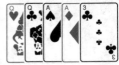

Identical hands of two pairs tie.

9 One pair
one pair of cards of the same rank plus three odd cards

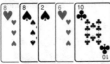

In two hands, the pair of the higher rank wins.

Ks outrank Js and win.

If the pairs are of the same rank, the highest ranking odd card wins.

The hands are identical except for one of their odd cards. Since 6 outranks 2, the hand with the 6 wins.

Identical hands tie.

10 High card

any hand of five odd cards, which are neither in
sequence nor make any of the hands already described

If there are two high-card hands, the one with the
highest ranking card wins.

Ace is the highest ranking card. The hand with the ace
wins.

If the highest cards in two high-card hands are of the
same rank, the next highest in rank among the other
odd cards wins.

If all cards match by rank, the hands tie.

Use of wild cards

A wild card can be used to represent or duplicate a card of any rank and suit, including itself.

Any card or group of cards can be declared wild before a game begins.

The most common wild cards

1 one or two jokers

2 one, two or four of the deuces

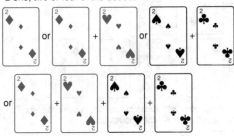

3 occasionally, one, two or four of the 3s, in combination with **1** or **2** above (some are shown below)

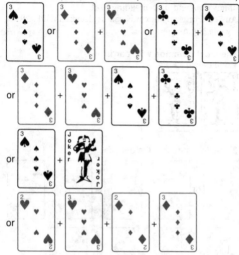

4 court cards with a design feature in common, such as one-eyed Js or Ks with moustaches

Ranking of hands using wild cards

There are two additions to the ten standard Poker hands
already described.

Five of a kind. This is any five cards of the same rank
value, one of which will, of course, be a wild card. This
hand ranks highest of all the hands, even above the
royal flush.

Five of a kind in Ks

 or other wild card

Double-ace flush. Ranking between full house and
flush, this hand has five cards of the same suit made up
of the ace, a wild card and any three other cards of the
same suit as the ace.

A double-ace flush in clubs

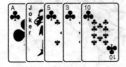

The rank of the twelve Poker hands with wild cards is as follows:

1 Five of a kind (highest rank)
2 Royal flush
3 Straight flush
4 Four of a kind
5 Full house
6 Double-ace flush
7 Flush
8 Straight
9 Three of a kind
10 Two pairs
11 One pair
12 High card. This is the lowest rank if nobody happens to be dealt a wild card. Since 12 cannot be made when any player has a wild card, the lowest ranking hand when wild cards are in play would be 11.

Draw Poker

Sometimes called Closed Poker, Draw Poker has some
variations of its own. It is the standard form of Poker
which preceded all other games.

Draw Poker is the Poker most often enjoyed as a family
game.

Players

Up to ten people can play, although two to six make the
best game. There should be no more than six when
playing for high stakes.

Cards

A standard deck of 52 cards is used. Two packs with
different backs may be used alternately, whenever a
player calls for a change of cards.

The pot

The centre of the table is the place where chips are
placed when they are put into the pot. This enables
everyone to see clearly how much is in the pot.

Aim

Players try to hold a higher ranking hand than any other
player at the showdown, thus winning the pot.

Preparing

Preliminaries are the same as for Basic Poker. Players
should also agree as to which type of ante and which of
the stake limits they are playing during the whole game.

The ante

There are two types of ante:

1 Ante paid by all the players. Before the deal and
beginning with the leader (the player to the dealer's left),
each player in turn places the same amount into the pot.

2 Dealer's edge. Only the dealer antes the pot.

Optional stake limits

There are five popular betting limits.

1 A specified minimum and maximum. Examples of such limits are: a 5p to 10p limit; 10p to 25p; 10p to 50p; 25p to £1, and so on.

The ante is usually the minimum.

Each player cannot bet higher than the maximum or lower than the minimum but can bet any amount in between the two.

2 Three-figure limits. In this instance limits could be: 5p, 10p and 15p. The first figure is the amount of the ante and the opening stake. After the draw, stakes must be either 10p or 15p.

The same rules apply to any three-figure limits agreed.

3 Jackpot. This is used when options **1** or **2** have been agreed but all players have passed on the first deal. Before starting the second deal, the dealer announces the amount in the pot, i.e. the total ante.

This then becomes the maximum stake that any player can make during that hand, unless it is lower than the maximum limit.

4 Pot limit. Players can stake any amount up to the total amount in the pot. If players want to raise the stakes, the pot total is calculated after adding the amount required for them to stay in the game.

5 Table stakes. This is a less popular option. Players each place whatever amount they choose on the table, above an agreed minimum. Usually there is no maximum.

Players may add to or subtract from their table stake after the showdown and before the next deal.

In turn, each player can stake up to – but not more than – the amount he or she has on the table.

A player whose table stake is less than the previous bettor has staked is allowed to play for the pot. (See **Some rules for Draw Poker: 3 Tapping out,** on p. 144.)

6 No limit. Poker with no limits to the stakes is rarely played.

Dealing

Starting with the leader and proceeding clockwise round to the dealer, players are dealt one card at a time, face down, until each has five cards.

The remaining cards are placed face down in a pile in front of the dealer. This stock will later be used for the draws.

Playing

Everyone examines their cards.

The leader begins. If holding a pair of Js or a pair of a higher rank, the leader may open the pot or pass. If not holding any such pairs, the leader must pass.

If the leader passes, the next player, seated clockwise, has the same two options, and so on.

Opening the pot

The person who makes the first stake is said to open the pot. The opener may or may not be the first player, because whoever opens the pot must hold in hand a pair of Js or a pair of a higher rank.

This rule enables players to use their skills by knowing the opener holds a high-ranking pair.

The opener places a bet in the pot, within the limits already agreed.

A player holding a pair of Js or higher is not compelled to play.

Opening the pot

Six members of the family are playing and the stake limit they have chosen is one to five chips.

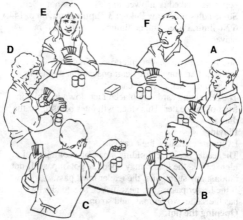

A Mum is the leader. She does not have a pair of Js. She passes.

B John cannot open. He passes.

C Dad holds a pair of Qs. He opens the pot with three chips.

D Gran can now choose to drop out, play or raise Dad's bet.

E Jill is already watching the events carefully.

F Uncle Tom is also the dealer. He will play after Jill, then Mum will have her turn again.

Splitting the opening pair

The player making the opening bet may split the pair of cards in hand, discarding one or both of the pair and keeping them to one side.

If the opener wins the showdown, he or she will have to show these cards.

Continuing play

If nobody opens the pot, because nobody holds a pair of Js or higher, then the deal ends.

Everyone antes again (unless dealer's edge is being played, in which case only the dealer antes).

The deal passes clockwise; the new dealer collects, shuffles, cuts and deals the cards again.

Play after the pot has been opened

When the pot is open, each player has three options and declares which one is being chosen:

1 Pass. Passing after the pot is open means dropping out, so the player folds up his or her cards face down in the centre of the table, forming a discard pile, and takes no further part in that deal.

2 Play. In this option the player must put a stake, equal to the opening bet, into the pot.

3 Raise. To raise, the player must stake the same amount as the opening player, plus an additional amount.

Play after the stake has been raised

Each player still has three options:

1 to pass by folding up his or her cards onto the discard pile and dropping out;

2 to play by staking the total of the raised bet. A player who has already placed a bet equal to the opening bet need only add the amount raised; or

3 to re-raise by staking the total of the raised bet plus an additional amount.

Completing the betting

Play continues for as many rounds as necessary, with

Result when the betting is completed

Dad (**C**) was the opener with three chips.
Gran (**D**) raised the stake to five chips.
Jill (**E**) passed and folded.
Uncle Tom (**F**) passed and folded. He remains as dealer and conducts the draw.
Mum (**A**) played, staking five chips.
John (**B**) played, staking five chips.
There are now a total of eighteen chips in the pot.

each player passing, playing or re-raising, until
everyone has stopped raising.

If all but one player has dropped out, that player wins
and claims the pot.

If the winner was the opener, that player's pair of Js or
higher pair must be shown.

If the winner was not the opener, that player does not
show any cards.

The draw

When there are two or more players remaining, they
participate in the draw.

Players should watch their opponents' decisions and
reactions closely during the draw to assess the strength
of their hands.

Beginning with the nearest active player to the left and
going clockwise in turn, the dealer asks each active
player 'how many' that player wants to draw. A player
has two options:

1 to stand pat, i.e. keep the five cards. The dealer then
passes on to the next player; or

2 to draw up to three cards.

A player choosing to draw must discard, face down, the
same number of cards before the dealer draws the new
cards from the top of the stock, dealing them face
down.

Once cards are discarded they cannot be retaken.

Mistakes

If the dealer shows a draw card by mistake, it is placed
face up to one side and is not used in play again until
the next deal. The dealer draws a replacement card.

If a player, or the dealer when making his or her own
draw, reveals a card, the card still stands.

If a player does not get the correct number of draw cards, the dealer must correct the mistake, unless a card has already been drawn and given to the next player. Players should check they have the correct number immediately.

Four players in the draw

Tom (**F**) asks Mum (**A**) 'how many'?
Mum says 'three' and discards three cards, replacing them with the three draw cards.
John (**B**) will draw one card.
Dad (**C**) and Gran (**D**) both watch everyone's reactions carefully.

The stock pile

If there are nine or ten players and the stock cards run out before everyone has completed the draw, the discards are collected, shuffled, cut and used to complete the draw.

Placing further stakes after the draw

Beginning with the player who opened the pot, and going round clockwise in turn, each player now has six options:

1 Pass. Passing players fold up their cards and drop out of play, leaving their stakes in the pot.

2 Check. Players can check their cards only if nobody has already made a bet.

By saying 'check', the player stays in the game and reserves the right to pass, bet, raise, re-raise or call at the next turn.

3 Bet. If nobody else has already bet, a player can make the first bet after the draw, staking any amount within the agreed limits for the game.

4 Raise. When the first bet has been made, players can then raise the stake as before.

5 Re-raise. When a raise has been staked, a player may re-raise, as before.

6 Call (leading straight to a showdown). A player calls another player to reveal his or her hand by paying into the pot the same stake as the player being called has bet. The challenging player says 'I call you' while paying in the stake.

The player who has been called must reveal his or her hand as it is the first of the showdown.

Four active players after the draw

Dad (**C**) starts, because he was the opener. He passes and folds.

Gran (**D**) checks, remaining an active player.

Mum (**A**) bets and places two chips in the pot.

John (**B**) raises Mum three and places five chips in the pot.

The call

Now there are only three active players: Gran, John and Mum. Gran realizes she can't win, so she passes and folds.

Mum adds three chips to the pot, to make her stake

equal to John's. Then she calls John to show his hand.
He has a 9-high straight flush.

John's hand

Mum then shows her hand. She wins with a Q-high
straight flush.

Mum's hand

The showdown
Players continue the betting round after the draw until
there is a showdown, which occurs in one of three
situations, as follows:

1 When all players pass, there is a showdown. The
original opener is first to show his or her hand; the rest
then follow in clockwise order. The highest ranking
hand wins the pot.

2 When one or more players call another player by
betting amounts to equal that raised by the latter, the
called player declares the rank of his or her hand first,
and shows it. The rest then follow in clockwise order.
(See the example when Mum calls John.)
The highest ranking hand wins the pot.

3 When a player has made a bet but nobody else bets, raises or calls, that player collects the pot without showing his or her hand, unless he or she was the opener, in which case the original pair of cards must be shown.

Some rules for Draw Poker

There are many advanced books on the subject of Poker and its rules. The four most basic rules are described below.

1 Declaring the wrong rank. If a player makes a mistake and declares his or her hand to be of a higher or lower rank than it actually is, the mistake can be put right if noticed immediately. However, if the pot has already been collected before the mistake is noticed, it must stand.

2 Five cards at showdown. If players have more or less than the required five cards in hand at the showdown, their hands are declared dead and they take no part in the showdown. They also lose their stakes.

3 Tapping out. A player who is running out of cash or chips is allowed to play up to the size of the pot until his or her chips run out. This is called a tap-out.

Bets made by any other player after someone has tapped-out are placed to one side.

At the showdown, if the tapped-out player wins, he or she can claim only the original pot and can continue in the game with the won chips.

If the tapped-out player loses at the showdown, he or she has no chips and cannot take part in the game.

4 Discards. Cards that are put on the discard pile, in exchange for cards drawn, must not be seen by anyone. The discard pile may not be inspected.

DRAW POKER VARIATIONS

There are so many variations that only a small selection of those in more regular use are described here.

Unless otherwise specified, all these variations have the same basic rules of Draw Poker.

Dealer's Choice

This version is often played in private homes where a regularly scheduled game takes place.

Each dealer, in turn, has the choice of naming which variation is to be played. People often invent their own slight variations, too.

The dealer describes the variation so that everyone is clear on the rules before the deal.

Deuces Wild

All or some of the 2s are wild cards; it should be agreed which.

The wild 2s can duplicate any card, including one already held by a player.

With so many wild cards, players may find themselves able to call more than one ranking of hands with the same cards. Players should therefore be careful not to call a lower ranking hand than is possible with their cards because – in this variation – the first-called hand stands.

Sample hands in Deuces Wild

This hand can be called as four 10s.

deuces duplicate as 10s

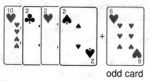 +

odd card

Or it can be called as a 10-high straight flush.

deuces duplicate as 9, 8 and 7

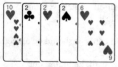

A straight flush is a higher ranking Poker hand than a four of a kind.

English Draw Poker
This is played exactly as standard Draw Poker, except at the draw, when the leader is allowed to draw four cards. The maximum draw for all other players is three, as in standard Draw Poker.

Joker Wild
One or more jokers may be added to the deck in this version. Jokers can stand for any card in the pack. The more jokers there are, the less strategic skill is needed.

Blind Openers
In this version, any player, holding any hand, may open the pot; a pair of Js or better is not needed.

Leading Blind Opener
In this game, the leading player always opens the pot, regardless of what hand is held.

Straight Draw Poker
Any player may open the pot with a blind opener in this game, and players may draw up to five cards each at the draw.

Poker with a Five-card Draw Buy
Players are allowed to draw up to five cards.

Spanish (or European) Draw Poker
This version differs from standard Draw Poker in two ways:
a only two to five people play, four being the best number; and
b the standard 52-card pack is stripped of all cards below the 7s, leaving a deck of 32 cards for play, which includes the aces.

Pass-out Draw Poker
This is sometimes called Bet or Drop. Players may only bet or drop out of the game; they may not check.

Progressive Draw Poker
This is an interesting variation of the conditions required for opening the pot.
If everyone passes on the first deal, then two Qs, or a higher pair, are needed to open the pot on the second deal.

Openers on the second deal

If all players continue to pass at the deals, the pair of cards required to open the pot changes in sequence, as shown here.

Openers on the third deal

Openers on the fourth deal

Openers on the fifth deal

as at the third deal

Openers on the sixth deal

    as at the second deal

Openers on the seventh deal

as at the first deal

If the pot is still unopened, the whole process is repeated.

Since there is an ante before each deal, there can be a very large pot before anyone makes the opening bet. Once the pot has been opened, the game is played exactly as Draw Poker. The process starts all over again in the next deal, i.e. Js or higher are required to open the pot.

Fives and Tens

In this variant, also known as Woolworth Draw or St Louis Draw, all 5s and 10s are wild cards.

The player opening the pot must hold one 5 and one 10. Antes and deals continue until someone is dealt the required cards.

High-low Draw Poker Variations

All these variations follow the standard Draw Poker rules with the exceptions given.

LOWBALL

This variation is Draw Poker in reverse. The aim is to hold the lowest hand at the showdown.

Cards

Ace is low and counts as 1.

A wild joker is often used, known as the 'bug'.

Openers

Any player can open the pot with any kind of hand.

Rank of hands in Lowball

Flushes and straights do not count. The lowest ranking hand is 5, 4, 3, 2, ace; it is known as a 'bicycle' or 'wheel'.

Each hand shown would win over any hand below it in numerical order (the two hands in 1 are tied). The suit is irrelevant; only the number value of the cards counts. The hand with the joker always ties with the hand it imitates.

Sample Lowball hands in rank order

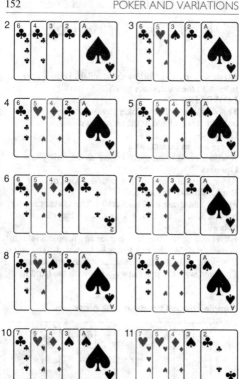

DOUBLE-BARREL DRAW

This game is played exactly as Draw Poker. However, if nobody opens the pot and everyone passes on the first round, then the game converts into Lowball Draw Poker on the second round. If all players pass once more, a new deal is dealt and the game reverts to Draw Poker.

HIGH-LOW DRAW POKER

In this variation the winning hands at the showdown are the highest and the lowest hands; the pot is split between them.

Anyone can open the pot with any hand.

The hands are ranked as in standard Draw Poker and the ace can be high or low.

LEG POKER

What is called 'playing for two legs' can be a challenging addition to any Poker game, but particularly to Draw Poker and its variations.

The first player to win at the showdown may not take the pot until winning again, i.e. winning a second leg.

The consequences of playing for two legs are:

a several players may win a first leg before someone wins two legs; and

b the pot can increase to a considerable sum.

In High-Low Draw Poker, the competition can be quite fierce, since two players win each game. A player does not have to win two high or two low legs, but can win with one of each.

NINE-HANDED HIGH-LOW DRAW POKER

This variation of High-Low Draw is for seven, eight or nine players.

The game

The deal is the same as in Draw Poker.

The leader must open the pot – with a blind opening or otherwise – but may check after the discard.

The number of raises in this and following rounds is limited to three.

The next round

Each remaining active player in turn either stands pat (by keeping all cards) or discards one or two cards.

Nobody draws any cards to replace the discards.

When everyone has played, the dealer then deals the next two cards from the deck face up into the centre of the table.

Sample situation after the discard round

1 Pass   2 Active player two discards   3 Pass

4 Active player stand pat – no discards

9 Pass

two centre cards

+ coin on it
first

second

8 Active player stand pat

7 Active player two discards   6 Pass   5 Active player one discard

The dealer places a chip on the first card dealt, to identify it. Both centre cards remain on the table during the game.

Players who discard one card 'replace' their discard with the first centre card – i.e., they hold only four cards in hand, but the fifth card is represented by the first centre card. Similarly, players who discard two cards 'replace' their discards with both centre cards – i.e., they hold only three cards in hand, but the other two cards that make up the hand are represented by the two centre cards. Thus, several players may 'hold' the same cards – the centre cards – at one time.

Continuing play

There is another betting round followed by the showdown.

High-low winners

Any hand counts. The players with the lowest and the highest hands are joint winners and share the pot. Straights and flushes can be high or low.

ROCKLEIGH

This is an intriguing High-low variation.

The deal

Each player is dealt only four cards.

The dealer then deals four pairs of cards face down in a row down the centre of the table.

After the first betting round, the dealer turns up any pair, leaving them visible during the second betting round.

This process continues, with the dealer continuing to turn up any pair, until all four pairs are turned up.

Rockleigh betting rounds

First betting round

Second betting round

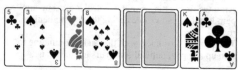

Third betting round

Fourth betting round

Fifth and final betting round

The showdown

Players declare their high or low hand using the best five cards selected from six available, i.e. the four in hand and the two in any one of the upturned pairs. Players wishing to declare both high and low can use one two-card group for high and one for low. A single two-card group may also be used for both high and low.

A sample hand

Cards on table

Cards in hand

Player rejects Q of diamonds and, without taking the cards from the table, selects the pair: 2 of spades and 4 of hearts.

in hand

on table

in hand

on table

in hand

Using ace low, the player declares the hand low.

SPIT IN THE OCEAN

There are dozens of Spit Poker variations that can be played using standard Draw Poker rules or with High-low rules. Spit in the Ocean is the basic spit variation.

Spit rules

Everyone is dealt four cards, then a final card is dealt face up on the table. This is to be the fifth card in every player's hand. It may not be rejected.

Playing

The game proceeds as in standard Draw Poker, except that the player to the left of the dealer must open the pot, regardless of what cards are in hand.

The showdown

Players should hold only four cards. The hand they declare depends on the game being played: Standard, Lowball or High-low Draw Poker.

Stud Poker

This is the fastest and most skilled version of Poker. It is also known as Open Poker and is preferred by those who play primarily for money. The pots can be quite large because there are more betting rounds than in Draw Poker.

Draw Poker is more favoured for games among friends and family members. However, learning to play some of the Stud Poker variations can improve a player's strategic skills.

Preparations

All the preliminaries, such as choosing the dealer and sitting positions and agreeing the stake limits and rank of cards, are the same as in Basic Poker.

Stake limits in Stud Poker

Below is a selection of six of the many betting agreements used in Stud.

1 Fixed limits. A minimum and maximum chip or money stake are decided, such as 1 to 2; 1 to 5; 5 to 10; 5 to 20; 10 to 25; 50 to 100, etc.

A player may bet the minimum, the maximum or any amount between the two.

There is no ante and no dealer's edge.

2 Choice of two. One of two agreed stakes may be bet, such as 5 and 10; 5 and 25; 50 and 100, etc.

A player may only bet the higher of the two stakes when:

a holding an opening pair or better;

b it is the betting round before the fifth card is dealt;

c it is the final betting round before the showdown.

3 Choice of three. One of three agreed stakes can be bet, such as one of 5, 10 and 20; or one of 10, 20 and 30.

A player must only bid the smallest or the middle stake, up to and including the fourth round of betting, unless holding an opening pair.

The maximum can be staked once the player holds an opening pair or has reached the final round of betting.

4 Dealer's edge. Before the deal, the dealer places into the pot an agreed amount, usually the minimum limit.

5 Player's ante. Before the deal everyone antes the minimum stake into the pot. The amount may be higher by mutual agreement.

Player's ante

6 Pot limit. The quickest way of betting is to begin
with a small ante from all players. Then, for each bet,
players choose how much to bet up to the maximum
already in the pot.

FIVE-CARD STUD POKER

After the ante, if appropriate, each player is dealt one
card face down. This is called the 'hole' card and
players carefully guard it from the eyes of the others.
In Stud Poker, the hole card is the only card not seen by
any player other than its owner.

Each player is then dealt one card face up on the table
and the remaining deck is placed face down in front of
the dealer.

The face-up cards are often called upcards.

First betting round

The player with the highest ranking upcard must open
the betting. If two or more players have upcards of the
same rank, the player nearest the dealer's left begins.
All the other players then bet in clockwise order.

Each player has four options:

1 to drop out, by calling 'out' and placing their two
cards face down on the table to begin a discard pile;

2 to play, by calling 'stay' and putting the same stake
into the pot as the opener;

3 to raise the pot, for example by two, and calling 'raise
two', which means putting in the pot the same amount
as the opener plus two more units; or

4 to re-raise the pot, by raising on an already raised bet.

End of first betting round

This happens when either of the following occurs:

a only one player remains active, in which case that
player claims the pot and does not have to reveal his or

her hole card. In this situation, a completely new deal
would take place; or

b the last bet in the pot has been met by all remaining
active players. Meeting a bet means betting the same
amount as the last bet, whatever it was.

When the round ends with **b**, each player is dealt a third
card face up on the table. The dealer does this, and
subsequent deals, by taking one card at a time from the
top of the deck, using only one hand, without picking
up the deck.

Second betting round

The player with the highest ranking pair of upcards
starts play. This player has three options:

1 to drop out by calling 'out' and throwing all cards on
the discard pile;

2 to check, by calling 'check', which means staying in
the game but not betting at the moment. A player
cannot check after a bet has been made; or

3 to bet, by placing a bet in the pot.

After someone has opened the betting, each following
player must do one of the following:

a stay and meet the bet, by putting an equal bet into the
pot;

b drop out, by discarding all cards;

c raise the bet; or

d re-raise the bet.

Any player who may have checked prior to a bet having
been made must adhere to rules **a** to **d**.

This betting round proceeds, as before, until:

a all but one player has dropped out;

b there remain two or more active players who have
met all bets; or

c nobody has opened the betting but two or more players have checked.

The dealer then deals each person a fourth card, face up, as before.

Third betting round

This is played the same as the second betting round. If two or more active players remain, they are dealt their fifth and final card, face up.

Fourth and last betting round

This is played the same as the previous two rounds, except that the option to play is now the call hand, i.e. players call their hands as they make their bets, starting with the player with the highest ranking four upcards. Players must also call possible flushes and straights.

The ranking of the hands is the same as for Basic Poker.

Showdown

Starting from the dealer's left and proceeding

clockwise, each active player in turn must turn over their hole card and declare the rank of their hand. The player with the highest ranking hand wins the pot. The game then proceeds in the same way until the time limit (agreed upon at the start) is reached. See Basic Poker for details of agreed limits.

STUD POKER VARIATIONS

There are many variations of Stud, and many of the variations have their own variations. People who play together regularly often invent their own supplementary rules. If this is done, they are best written down to prevent arguments later.

Some variations are described here.

Five-card Stud with Deuces Wild

All the 2s are wild cards. Players must declare at the showdown the value attributed to any wild cards they hold. They cannot change their declaration after their turn has passed.

Sometimes a joker is added as an extra wild card.

Five-card Stud with Last Card Down

This is played as before but with the last card dealt face down so players have two hole cards.

Five-card Stud with Five Bets

In this variation, an extra betting round is inserted after the hole cards have been dealt and before the first upcard is dealt. This means that the first betting round is done on knowledge of one card only.

Skeets

This version is played exactly as Five-card Stud but after each betting round the dealer has the option of calling 'skeets' and dealing a spit card to the centre of the table.

Any player can include one or more of the spit cards to make the best hand at the showdown.

Sample Stud Poker hands

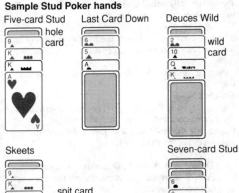

Five-card Stud

Last Card Down

Deuces Wild

Skeets

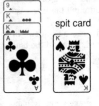

spit card

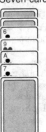

Seven-card Stud

Buy-ins

In this option, after the fifth betting round the dealer calls 'buy one' or 'substitution'.

Each player in turn may buy a card from the dealer by discarding one and then being dealt a new card. If a hole card is substituted, the new card is dealt face down; if an upcard, the new card is dealt face up.

The dealer calls three buy-ins by calling 'buy one', 'buy two' or 'buy three' accordingly.

The cards are paid for as follows:

a first buy-in costs one times the minimum betting limit;

b second buy-in costs two times the minimum betting limit;

c third buy-in costs three times the minimum betting limit.

Six-card Stud

This is played as Five-card Stud but with a sixth card dealt face down to form the second hole card.

Players use the best five out of their hand to make a Poker hand at the showdown.

Seven-card Stud

Also known as Peek Poker, Down the River or Seven-toed Pete, Seven-card Stud is overtaking the five-card version in popularity.

Before the first betting round, players are dealt two hole cards, one at a time, and one upcard. After all the betting rounds, players are dealt a final hole card.

Players use their best five cards to make their hands for the showdown.

Two-leg Stud

In Two-leg Stud the winner has to make winning hands twice to claim the pot. They do not have to be made consecutively.

Heinz

This is a Seven-card Stud game in which all 5s and 7s are wild cards. A player being dealt an upcard that is wild must meet the pot or drop out.

Rollover

Also known as Beat Your Neighbour or No Peekie, this game is similar to Seven-card Stud except that players are dealt seven face-down cards, one at a time, which they do not examine.

Players each shuffle their seven cards in a pile, face down on the table, without looking at them.

The leader begins by rolling over his or her top card face up on the table and bets on it. All players bet in turn as in Stud Poker.

The next player in turn, in clockwise order, then rolls over his or her cards, beginning with the top card in the pile, until a card is revealed that is higher in rank than the card of the previous player.

That player, and the others, again bet in turn.

Players continue, in turn, to roll over their cards and bet.

A player who runs out of cards without rolling over a higher ranking card has to drop out of the game and discard his or her cards.

This process continues until one player remains with an unbeatable hand and claims the pot.

Rollover sample hands with four players
leader

Leader rolls over one card and there is a betting round.

second player

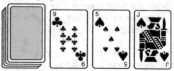

J of spades beats 10 of hearts, so another betting round ensues.

third player

The third player cannot beat the J of spades, so there is not another betting round.

fourth player

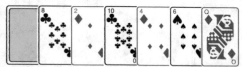

Q of diamonds beats J of spades, so there is another betting round.

first player

K of spades beats Q of diamonds, so there is another betting round.

second player

The second player cannot beat the K of spades, so there is not another betting round.

The third player cannot roll over any more cards, and so is out.

fourth player

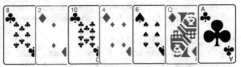

Ace of clubs is unbeatable, so the fourth player wins.

Anaconda

This is a Seven-card Stud variation.

Each player is dealt seven cards face down, singly.

Players examine their cards and there is a betting round.

Then each player passes any three cards to the player on the left. This is done simultaneously on the command of the dealer.

Another betting round takes place.

Then each player passes two cards to the left, and there is a third betting round.

Each player then passes one card to the left and there is a final betting round before a rollover starts.

(Sometimes the passing of two and then one card is omitted.)

Players then choose their five best cards and put these in any order they like and place them face down on the table.

On a given signal by the dealer, everyone rolls over their top card.

A betting round then takes place, starting with the player with the highest ranking upcard.

Another card is then rolled over by the active players, and another betting round ensues, and so on.

If played as a High-low Stud Game (see below), then players must declare their hands high or low at the last betting round before the showdown, when each player still has one face-down card. High and low hands share the pot.

HIGH-LOW STUD GAMES

Any Stud Poker game can be played as Lowball Stud or High-low Stud. For details see High-low Draw Poker Variations, p. 151.

Other Poker Games

POKER SOLITAIRE

This is a time-consuming game for two or more players.

There are no antes, no betting rounds and no draw.

Players pay the winner according to a points system.

Scoring

Pencil and paper are essential for scoring.

There are two scoring systems: American and English, described below. It should be agreed which is to be used. The monetary value of 1 point should also be agreed.

Poker hands

Nine standard Poker hands are each given a points value. In the American system, points match their standard ranking. In the English system, points value depends on the ease or difficulty of making the hand.

Values of Poker hands

Hand	American value	English value
Royal flush	100	30
Straight flush	75	30
Four of a kind	50	16
Full house	25	10
Flush	20	5
Straight	15	12
Three of a kind	10	6
Two pairs	5	3
One pair	2	1

Sample deal in progress

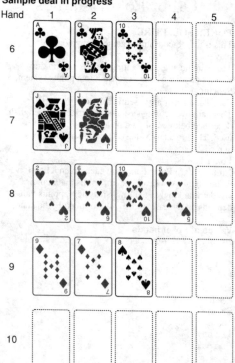

Playing

A draw is made, which determines who begins play.
Each player, in turn, shuffles the whole pack of 52
cards and deals themselves 25 cards, face up on the
table in five rows of five cards (a grid), each row and
column being one Poker hand, to make ten hands in all.
The player must choose carefully where to place each
card as it is dealt, the aim being to make the five best
possible hands.

A card can be put anywhere in the five-by-five grid, but
once it has been placed on the table it cannot be moved
elsewhere.

When the player has dealt 25 cards, his or her scores
are listed and totalled.

The next player now begins his or her deal.

Winning

When all players have dealt, points scores are
compared. The highest score wins.

All the other players then deduct their own scores from
the winner's score and pay the difference to the winner.

POKER SQUARES

This is a faster and more competitive variation of Poker
Solitaire.

Each player needs a deck of cards. Plenty of table space
will be required.

The game is scored as in Solitaire, but everyone plays
with the same 25 cards.

Dealing

The dealer shuffles his or her deck while the others sort
their decks into suit sequence for easy access.

The dealer plays as in Solitaire but calls out the name
of each card as it is dealt.

All the other players have to take the same card from their decks and play it on the table at the same time. Each tries to make the best ten hands.

Winning

Scores and payment are the same as in Solitaire.

LEFTY LOUIE

This is a wild-card variation that can be used with any Poker game.

All picture cards whose characters are looking to the left are wild cards.

This gets interesting when two different packs are used during a game, as the way picture cards are printed varies from pack to pack.

Choosing a familiar pack of cards gives a player an advantage over the other players.

Sample of wild cards from one pack

STRIP POKER

This is a fast version of Poker in which the stake is not chips but clothing!

What will count as an item of clothing, and the limit to stripping, should be agreed upon before play begins.

The rules are as for Draw Poker but without an ante or any betting.

After the draw, all the players turn their cards face up on the table. The person with the lowest ranking hand is required to take off a piece of clothing.

Strip Poker in progress

USING A STRIPPED DECK
The speed and skill of any Poker game can be increased by using a stripped deck of cards. No cards are wild.
The 40-card deck
In this deck, all the 2s, 3s and 4s are stripped and the ace ranks high.
The 32-card deck
This deck is made by removing all the 2s, 3s, 4s, 5s and 6s. Ace ranks high. This deck makes for a very fast game. High stakes are frequently placed.

The 'Italian' deck
This is a 40-card deck made by stripping all the 8s, 9s
and 10s. Ace can rank high or low.

The Italian deck

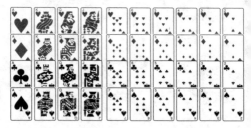

WILD WILD POKER
The wildest and most hectic games of Poker are those
in which wild cards are chosen by the players during
the game.

Players new to Wild Wild Poker should keep the stakes
low until they become familiar with the effects these
wild cards have on their chosen variation of Poker.

Any Card Wild
This is the wide-open version in which each player can
make any one of the cards in hand into a wild card,
declaring which is the wild card at the showdown.

In another version, players declare immediately after
the deal which card in their hands they are making into
a wild card.

The rank of these cards is written down, because all

other cards of the same rank automatically become wild cards.

In this version of Any Card Wild, one of every player's cards is known.

If there are four players, there would be 16 wild cards; if there are seven players, the number of wilds jumps to 28.

Sample wild cards in an Any Card Wild game with four players

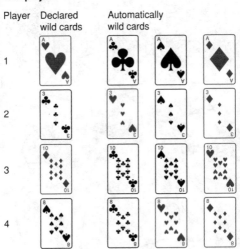

Player	Declared wild cards	Automatically wild cards		
1	A♥	A♣	A♠	A♦
2	3♣	3♥	3♠	3♦
3	10♦	10♣	10♠	10♥
4	8♠	8♣	8♥	8♦

Any Suit Wild
In this version, known also as Hectic Poker, any suit is
wild, making 13 cards into wild cards.
Either all players agree before the deal which suit is to
be wild for the hand, or each player can declare his or
her own wild suit at the showdown.

The card games in this chapter need not be competitive but can be fun to play at home for points, chips or small stakes.

Commit

This is a version of Comet, said to have been named after the sighting of Halley's Comet in 1759. There are similarities between both these games and the game of Fan Tan, also described in this section.

Comet is a game of chance with a large element of skill.

Players

Any number of players from three to seven can play. Eight or more can play if two decks are used.

Cards

The 8 of diamonds is removed from a standard deck of 52 cards, leaving 51 cards in play. They are ranked with ace low up to K high with the exception of the 9 of diamonds (see **Playing** on p. 180).

Chips

Everyone should begin with a large supply of chips or counters. If they are to have monetary value, they should be worth very little because the losses and winnings in this game can be high.

Before the deal takes place, everyone antes the pot by putting one chip in it.

Dealing

A dealer, chosen by a cut of the deck, shuffles the cards and deals, beginning with the player on the left. The turn to deal moves to the left in subsequent hands.

Diamonds in rank order

high   low

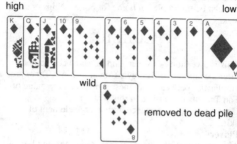

wild

removed to dead pile

The dealer deals all the cards out, one at a time to each player, until everyone has the same number. Any odd cards left over are placed face down in a dead pile. The number of odd cards varies with the number of players – for example:

three players: seventeen cards each and no odd cards
four players: twelve cards each and three odd cards
seven players: seven cards each and two odd cards
eight players: six cards each and three odd cards

If two decks are used, i.e. 102 cards, including two 9s of diamonds, then eight players would have twelve cards each and there would be six odd cards. This would make a more interesting game demanding more skill.

Aim

Each player tries to be the first to have no cards left in hand.

Playing

The person to the left of the dealer begins by putting

down any card face up on the table, such as the 6 of spades.

Though not compelled to, the player may then begin to build the 'tail of the comet' by adding as many cards as possible of the same suit in ascending order. For example, the player might add the 7, 8, 9 and 10 of spades.

Then the person holding the J of spades adds it – plus the Q and K, if holding them – to the sequence.

When a K is reached, the player who played it may start another suit sequence with any chosen card.

If a sequence is held up because nobody holds the next card, as it is in the dead pile, then the last player may begin a new sequence.

The 9 of diamonds

If a sequence has been stopped because no player holds the next card, the holder of the 9 of diamonds can play it to represent the card on which the sequence has become stuck. The sequence then 'leapfrogs' over the 9 of diamonds and continues as before, with the next card in order.

The 9 of diamonds can also represent itself and be used in a diamond sequence. How to use the 9 of diamonds is the choice of whoever holds the card.

The payoff

While the game is in progress, two chips are paid to the person who plays the 9 of diamonds. However, if a player is still holding the card when the game ends, he or she must pay everyone two chips each.

It is usual for the person who ends a sequence with the K to be paid one chip by the other players. Similarly, any player holding a K at the end of a game must pay everyone else one chip.

The first player to get rid of all his or her cards is the winner and collects all the chips in the pot.

Before the next deal, everyone antes the pot again.

Sample layout of a game in progress

first player   second player

stopped because 6 of diamonds in dead pile

next player starts new sequence

stopped because 6 of spades already on table

next player starts new sequence

Cuckoo

This is a version of Ranter Go Round suitable for children and adults.

Cards

A standard deck of 52 cards is used in which ace ranks low.

Rank

high   low

Preparations

From six to twenty people can play. Each should have three chips, small coins or matchsticks.

A dealer is chosen, who then shuffles the cards and deals each player one card face down.

Playing

The aim is to not get caught holding the lowest ranking card.

Starting with the player to the dealer's left, each person in turn chooses to call either 'stand' (keep the card) or 'change' (exchange the card with the player to the left).

Player **A** calls change.

Player **B** must give **A** his or her card unless it is a K. If player **B** has a K it is shown, and **A** must stand.

Although player **B** now has the right to stand or change, he or she would keep the K because it is the highest ranking card.

Player **C** then has the choice, and so on round the table.

Declaring cards

If a player passes an ace, 2 or 3, it must be declared.

The dealer

The dealer, in turn, can either stand or change. If changing, it must be done by cutting the remaining pack of cards and taking the top card from the cut. If a K is drawn, the dealer declares it but loses the hand.

Winning or losing the hand

After the dealer has played, but not drawn a K, everyone reveals their cards.

The player with the lowest ranking card loses one chip to the central pot.

Two or more equal losers all pay.

Play continued

A new hand of one card each is dealt by the next player on the left of the first dealer, i.e. player **A**. Then player **B** starts by choosing to stand or change.

Winning the game

The game continues, each person dealing in turn, until only one player – the winner – is left with chips. The winner then claims all the chips in the pot.

If there are eight players, the winner gains 21 chips plus his or her three original chips.

Stand or change

Fan Tan

Also known as Sevens, Parliament or Card Dominoes,
Fan Tan requires considerable skill and is a very simple
and enjoyable social and family game.

The banking version, known as Chinese Fan Tan, is a
game totally based on chance, requiring no skill at all
(see Section 4).

Players

Three to eight people can play. All players ante the pot
with one chip before the cards are dealt.

Chips

In a family game it is a good idea for everyone to
exchange low-value coins for large numbers of chips,
as the gains and losses can be quite high, despite the
skill involved.

This is an excellent game for children because they can
experience the excitement, and the reality, of gambling
without losing huge amounts of money.

Cards

A standard deck of 52 cards is used with aces ranking
low.

Rank

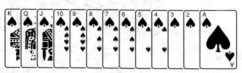

high   low

Sample layout of cards in play

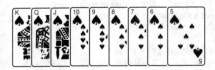

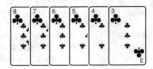

Aim

Players try to get rid of all their cards as quickly as
possible.

Dealing

Players cut for who shall be the first dealer, who then
shuffles and deals out all the cards, one at a time,
beginning with the player to the left and going
clockwise. Players deal in turn, in clockwise rotation.
Because all the cards are dealt, some players may have
one more card than others. Those with the advantage of
one fewer card should pay another chip into the pot
before play begins.

Playing

The first player to the left of the dealer begins by
playing a 7, if possible. If that player cannot play a 7,
the turn passes to the next player to the left, and so on
until a 7 is played. After a 7 has been laid down,
beginning a sequence, players can either:

a play the next card of the same rank in the sequence
order; or

b play a 7 to begin a new sequence.

Players who cannot play a card must pay one chip into
the pot, and the turn then passes to the next player.

The 7s are laid down in the centre of the table; a 6,
when played, goes on one side of the 7, and an 8 on the
other. Once a 6 or an 8 has been played, any player, in
turn, may play a card of the next lower rank (a 5 on the
6, or a card of the next higher rank (a 9 on the 8, and
so on as the new sequences are built.

Penalties

Players who pass when they could play must put three
chips into the pot.

Those who pass when they could play a 7 must also pay five chips to players who possess the 6 and 8 of the same suit.

Winning

The game continues, the cards being played up to the K and down to the ace in each suit until someone plays his or her last card and becomes the winner.

The game then stops and everyone left holding cards puts one chip for each card they hold into the pot.

The winner then takes all the pot.

The next game can then begin with the ante as before.

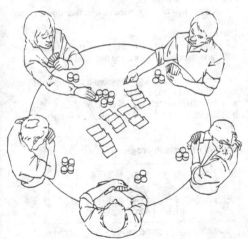

Go Boom

This is a simple game for two or more players, which very young children can also play. A standard deck of cards is used in which ace ranks high.

Aim

Players try to get rid of all their cards.

Dealing

Players cut for the deal. The highest cut deals seven cards, face down and one at a time in a clockwise direction, to each player.

The remaining cards are piled neatly, face down in the centre.

Playing

Everyone sorts their cards and the person to the dealer's left starts the round by placing one card face up on the table.

The next player (clockwise) places a face-up card on top of the first card. This card must be:

a of the same suit (all spades etc.); or

b of the same rank (number or picture) as the previous one.

Sample of game in progress

same suit   same rank   same suit

When players cannot follow suit or rank, they take cards from the top of the spare pile until a playable card turns up.

When everyone has played in that round, the person who played the highest ranking card leads the next. If there is a tie, the one who played the first highest ranking card starts the next round.

When the spare pile runs out, a player must say 'pass', and it is the next player's turn.

Winning the game

The winner is the one who gets rid of all his or her cards and shouts 'boom!' This is known as 'going boom'.

SCORING GO BOOM

In this variation points are scored for going boom, which makes the game more interesting. The player who goes boom scores points for every card still held by the other players as follows:

K, Q and J:	10 points each
ace:	1 point each
all other cards:	face value

Points value of cards

10 points each   face value   1 point

The first person to score a previously agreed number of points (usually 250) is the winner.

CRAZY EIGHTS

This variation is played in the same way as Go Boom but with the 8s used as wild cards which can be played on any card. The player then chooses which suit shall follow it.

The player who goes boom scores points for all the cards still held by the others, as follows:

8s: 50 points each
K, Q, J: 10 points each
aces: 1 point each
all other cards: face value

If the spare pile runs out before anyone goes boom, all players count the value of their cards, and the winner is the one with the lowest total. The winner then scores the difference between his or her own total and the combined total of the other players' scores.

Points values of cards

50   10 points each   1 point   4 points   9 points
points

I Doubt It

This is a fast and often hilarious game for up to twelve players of any age.

Competition

Players try to get rid of all their cards and consequently collect a chip for each card that others are still holding.

Cards and chips

The larger the group the more fun the game is, especially when two decks of cards are used.

Everyone will need about twenty chips or matchsticks.

Aim

At their turns, players must follow the sequence of cards put down, or successfully bluff if they do not hold the appropriate cards.

Dealing

A dealer is chosen and deals out all the cards. It does not matter that some players will have a different number of cards.

Playing

The player to the dealer's left begins, putting one to four cards (one to eight if two decks are used) face down on the table and declaring them. The declaration is the number of cards discarded and the type – for the first player, the type is aces, for the second it is 2s, and so on.

The first player puts down two cards, for example, and says 'two aces'.

What has been put down might be aces or it might be a bluff.

Anyone who thinks the player is bluffing can call a

challenge, saying 'I doubt it.' When more than one
player challenges, the first to speak is the challenger.
The last group of cards to be put down are then turned
over.

If it was a bluff, the player must pick up all the cards in
the discard pile.

If it was not a bluff, the challenger must pick up all the
discarded cards.

The next player in turn then puts down up to four (or up
to eight) cards, saying 'one 2', 'two 2s' etc.

The next calls 3s, the next 4s and so on in ascending
order of rank.

Continuing the round

When the K has been reached, and if all players still
have cards, the sequence begins again, with the next
player putting down aces, and so on.

Winning

The winner is the first player to get rid of all his or her
cards. The winning player then collects chips from each
player – one for each card the player still holds. When
players run out of chips they must drop out.

Strategy

Playing successfully can require skill and planning. It is
wise for every player to work out which cards they will
have to call on their turns (examples are given in the
tables opposite) and to dispose of unwanted cards early
in the game before the discard pile gets too big. Also,
challenging early in the game can give players more
cards in hand with which to follow the sequence.

Planning to bluff early and be 'honest' later in the game
– by not having to bluff – is a good strategy.

Facial expressions have a lot to do with success. If a

player can act as if the cards being discarded are a bluff, when they are actually 'honest', others will be encouraged to challenge and, as a result, pick up the entire discard pile.

Cards to be called in a five-player game

Player	Cards
first player (leader)	ace, 6, J
second player	2, 7, Q
third player	3, 8, K
fourth player	4, 9
fifth player (dealer)	5, 10

The fourth player would begin the next round by calling aces.

Cards to be called in a six-player game

Player	Cards
first player (leader)	ace, 7, K
second player	2, 8
third player	3, 9
fourth player	4, 10
fifth player	5, J
sixth player (dealer)	6, Q

The second player would begin the next round by calling aces.

Rummy

Internationally popular, Rummy is a social and a family game. It is the basis of more competitive games such as Gin Rummy, Knock Rummy and others that are found in Section 1.

Players

Two to six players can play. The number of cards dealt varies with the number of players.

Competition

Players try to collect points or counters from the other players by winning the hand. If it is decided to use counters, each player should start with about 100.

Cards

A standard deck of 52 cards is used. Ace ranks low.

Rank

high   low

Aim

Each player tries to get rid of all his or her cards by making melds and sequences.

Dealing

Cards are dealt as follows:

two players: ten cards each
three or four players: seven cards each
five or more players: six cards each

Everyone looks at their cards and sorts them.

The stock and the discard

The remaining cards form the stock and are placed face down in the centre. The top card from the stock is turned face up and placed beside the stock to form the discard pile.

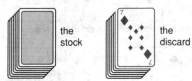

the stock

the discard

Playing

There are three stages in play.

1 The person to the left of the dealer begins by taking one card, either from the stock or from the discard. The aim is to pick up a card that might help to make melds (three or four cards of the same rank) and sequences (runs of three or four cards of the same suit).

2 The player may then lay down on the table, face up, any melds or sequences made from cards in hand. Laying down is not obligatory, but melds and sequences still in the hand when someone wins are a negative score. Players may add cards to their own and others' melds and sequences – this is known as 'laying off'.

3 At the end of the turn, provided the player has not melded or laid off all cards (see **Going rummy**), he or she throws away one card, which must not be the one just picked up from the discard.

If the stock pile runs out, the discard is turned face down, to make a new stock, and the top card is turned up as the new discard.

Sample melds and sequences

meld of three 10s

meld of four aces

sequence of
three clubs

sequence of four diamonds

Going rummy

A player may decide to risk going out all at once by melding all cards in one turn without previously having laid off or melded any. This is called 'going rummy', and it doubles the points won.

Winning the game

Each person plays in turn until someone 'goes out' by laying down all his or her cards. An odd card that cannot be placed may be discarded, but a discard is not essential when going out.

Counting points

Any cards remaining in the hand are counted at their face value. Ace counts as 1, and the court cards count as 10 each.

Paying counters

Players each declare their total points and pay the same
number of counters to the winner. If the winner has
'gone rummy', they pay double.

The game then continues, the dealership passing
clockwise, until all but one player have run out of
counters or a player reaches a previously agreed total of
points. In the former case, the winner's counters would
then total 100 times the number of players.

Some players prefer a time limit, when the player who
holds the most counters is the winner.

WILD-CARD RUMMY

This variation is played with the deuces as wild cards
which may be used in any meld or sequence.

meld with a wild card   sequence with two wild cards

Sometimes two jokers are added to the deck as extra
wild cards, which makes the game more exciting. All
wild cards have a value of 25 points.

There must always be more natural cards than wild
cards in any meld or sequence.

Aces can go 'round the corner', i.e. they can be both
high and low in a sequence, for example: K, A, 2, 3.

Nobody lays down any cards unless they can go out. To
win at Wild-card Rummy, a player must go out by
laying down all cards at once.

RUMMY-ROUND-THE-CORNER

In this variation the ace goes 'round the corner', as in Wild-card Rummy. When drawing, a player can draw the top stock card or the top discard. If drawing from the discard, the player then has the option of also drawing the top stock card or the next discard in the pile. As in regular Rummy, only one card can be discarded.

A player can only win by going out all at once.
The ace always counts as 11 points.

Aces 'round the corner'

ace high

ace low

ace 'round the corner'

Scotch Whist

Deceptively named, this game is not at all like Whist. It is often called Catch the Ten.

Players

Any number from two to six play for themselves. If there are four players, they might prefer to play in partnerships of two against two.

Cards

A standard deck of cards is stripped of all 2s, 3s, 4s and 5s to make a 36-card deck.

Ace ranks high in both trump and plain suits, with J ranking highest when a suit is trumps. A trick consists of one card from every person played in turn.

Rank when spades is a plain suit

high   low

Rank when spades are trumps

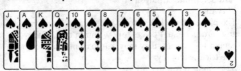

high   low

Aim

Players try to win as many tricks as possible, especially those which contain high-scoring trump cards.

Competition

Since the winner wins on points (see **Scoring** opposite), the competition is to score as many points as possible.

Dealing

The player who makes the highest cut is the first dealer. He or she shuffles the cards and asks the player on the right to cut them.

Beginning with the player on the left of the dealer and proceeding clockwise, the dealer deals cards singly, face down, to each player.

If there are two or three players, they are dealt ten cards each.

If there are more than three players, the whole deck is dealt out. With four players, each receives nine cards and the last card dealt to the dealer is turned up; it determines the trump suit for that hand.

Five players will be dealt seven cards each, and the last (36th) card will be turned up to determine trumps before being taken by the dealer, who will then have an eight-card hand.

Six players receive six cards each, and the dealer's final card determines trumps.

Playing

The player to the left of the dealer begins by playing any card in hand. Players follow suit in turn. If they cannot follow suit, they may trump or play any card.

The trick is won by:

a the highest trump card; or

b the highest card of the leading suit.

The player winning a trick takes all the cards in the trick, puts them to one side and leads to the next trick. Play continues in this way until every card has been played. If there are five players, the final trick will consist of six cards.

Scoring

At the end of a hand, when all cards have been played, players count their scores. Certain trump cards are worth points when won in tricks:

J of trumps: 11 points
10 of trumps: 10 points
ace of trumps: 4 points
K of trumps: 3 points
Q of trumps: 2 points

Players also score 1 point for every card taken in tricks in excess of the number each player was dealt. For example:

dealt nine, taken fifteen in tricks: scores 6 points
dealt seven, taken eighteen in tricks: scores 11 points

Players who fail to follow the rules of play are not allowed to score in that deal, and have 10 points deducted from their scores.

Winning the game

The first person to reach a score of 41 points wins the game. If two players each reach a total of 41 in the same hand, the winner is decided by scoring the points in this order: 10 of trumps, card points, ace, K, Q and J of trumps; again, the player with 41 points wins.

If there is no winner, all players lose their points and a new hand is played, and so on until one player reaches 41 points in a hand.

Seven-up

Seven-up is game for two or three players, in which the aim is to be the first to make 7 points by making tricks.

Cards

A standard deck of 52 cards is used, the ace ranking high.

Rank

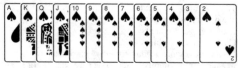

high   low

Dealing

Players cut for the deal. The one with the highest cut is the dealer and deals six cards, face down, to each player in two packets of three.

The next card is turned face up to indicate the trump suit. If it is any of the Js, the dealer wins 1 point.

Subsequent deals pass clockwise around the table.

The trump suit

The player to the dealer's left calls 'stand' if satisfied with the trump suit. Play then begins. If not satisfied, the player says 'I beg' and the dealer must choose to keep or to change trumps.

If keeping the trumps, the dealer replies 'take one'. The player who begged then scores 1 point and play begins.

If the dealer chooses to change trumps, the face-up card is put to one side and the dealer deals a packet of three more cards to each player, turning the next card up to indicate the new trump suit.

If it is the same suit as the first trump, then the dealer repeats the procedure of dealing another three cards to each player and turning up the next card.

If the extra deal produces a new trump suit, play begins. If this card is a J, the dealer wins a point, provided it is not of the same suit as the first trump.

The procedure can be repeated until a new trump is found. If the deck runs out before a new trump is turned up, the cards are thrown in, shuffled and redealt.

Discarding

After the trump has been changed, players must discard all but six cards from their hands.

Playing

Play is the same as Whist. The player to the left of the dealer plays one card to lead to the first trick. Players must each follow suit if possible. If not they may use a trump or discard.

The player who plays the highest trump wins the trick; if no trump is played, the one who plays the highest card of the leading suit wins the trick.

The winner of one trick leads to the next one. Play continues until all six tricks are made. Players claim their own tricks, keeping them nearby, face down.

Scoring

Tricks are turned face up for scoring at the end of each round. Points from tricks are won as follows:

a a 'high' earns 1 point to the player dealt the highest trump;

b a 'low' earns 1 point to the player dealt the lowest trump;

c a 'jack' earns 1 point to the player who takes the J of trumps in a trick;

d 'game' earns 1 point to the player who takes the highest total value of cards in tricks.

Value of cards

Cards each carry a points value as shown below. Only cards of these ranks are worth points.

Points values

| 4 points each | 3 points each | 2 points each | 1 point each | 10 points each |

Winning the game

The game is won by the first player to make 7 points. If two or more players reach 7 points in the same hand, the points of each are ranked in order, as follows, to decide who is the winner: high, low, jack, game. Again, the first to reach 7 points wins.

FOUR-HANDED SEVEN-UP

In this variation, four people play in pairs as partners sitting opposite to each other. Play proceeds as in the standard game except that the two players to the dealer's right may only look at their cards after the trump suit has been decided.

CALIFORNIA JACK

Sometimes called Draw Seven or California Loo, this variation is played by two people and has the following differences from the standard game.

Trumps

Trumps are always the first card turned up, but there is a new trump suit for each trick. First the winner, and then the loser, of each trick takes a card from the top of stock. The next card is then turned up to determine trumps for the next trick.

When the stock is exhausted, players continue making tricks, and using the last trump as trumps, until their cards are used up. The winner of one trick leads to the next.

Scoring

Each of the following, taken in tricks, scores 1 point:

the highest trump;

the lowest trump; and

the J of trumps.

The winner is the first player to scores 10 points.

Spoil Five

The cards in this game are ranked in a very unusual way. Counters or chips are used for scoring.

Players

The best number of players is five or six, although any number from two upwards can play. Each person plays individually.

Cards

A standard deck of 52 cards is used and the ranking changes according to suit and status. Ranking is as follows from high to low.

Spades and clubs

Plain: K, Q, J, ace, 2, 3, 4, 5, 6, 7, 8, 9, 10
Trumps: 5, J, ace of hearts, ace, K, Q, 2, 3, 4, 6, 7, 8, 9, 10

Diamonds

Plain: K, Q, J, 10, 9, 8, 7, 6, 5, 4, 3, 2, ace
Trumps: 5, J, ace of hearts, ace, K, Q, 10, 9, 8, 7, 6, 4, 3, 2

Hearts

Plain: K, Q, J, 10, 9, 8, 7, 6, 5, 4, 3, 2
Trumps: 5, J, ace, K, Q, 10, 9, 8, 7, 6, 4, 3, 2

When hearts is a plain suit, there is no ace because the ace of hearts always takes third rank in all trumps suits.

Aim

Players try to win three tricks and stop any other player from doing so.

The pool

Players agree on how many counters are to be put in the pool whenever a contribution is made. Before the first

Rank in trumps

spades (or clubs)

diamonds

hearts

deal, everyone puts in the same contribution.
The pool is won by the player who takes three tricks in one hand.

Dealing

Using standard ranking with ace high and 2 low, the players cut for deal. The lowest card determines the dealer. Beginning with the player to the dealer's left and moving clockwise, five cards are dealt face down to each player in packets of two then three or three then two. The next card is turned face up. Its suit determines trumps.

Rank in plain suits

spades (or clubs)

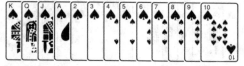

diamonds

hearts

Exchanging and robbing

When the upcard (denoting trumps) is an ace, the dealer
may 'rob' it by exchanging it for any card in hand
before the first card is led.

If the ace of trumps is dealt to a player, that player may
choose to exchange the upcard for any card in hand.

A player holding the ace of trumps must declare it at
his or her first turn if that player has not made an
exchange. Failure to declare means the ace

automatically ranks lowest of the trumps for that hand, even if it is the ace of hearts.

Playing

The player on the dealer's left begins by playing the leading card. Each person plays one card to each trick. The trick is won by the highest ranking card of the leading suit or of the trump suit if a trump is used. The winner leads to the next trick.

If the leading card is a plain suit, all players may choose to follow suit or trump but may only discard if they cannot do either.

If the lead is a trump card, players must follow suit if they can, but may 'renege' by holding back any of the top three trumps, providing the lead card was a lower trump.

Jinxing

A player who wins three tricks may take the pool and end the hand or may jinx, meaning play will continue and that player will try to win the remaining two tricks. If successful, that player takes the pool and from all players the same number of counters as each put into the pool.

Failure to take both tricks means the player loses the pool and the hand is counted a 'spoil'.

A spoil

A hand is called a spoil when nobody wins three tricks or the player who jinxes fails. The pool remains and the player to the left of the previous dealer makes the next deal. Only that player contributes to the pool. If there is no spoil, the pool is won and everyone puts counters in again.

4. BANKING GAMES

The games described in this section are played between the players and a banker. Casinos and clubs employ dealers who act as bankers, collecting and paying out betting chips as they are won and lost.

A casino dealer never surrenders the deal to anyone else.

In addition to dealers at each gaming table, casinos also have supervisors who watch the game and rule on any mistakes or disagreements.

In a private, social game, the banker/dealer can be one of the players, with each person taking the position in turn.

Some banking games described here require special table layouts.

The betting chips

In a casino or club, the chips may be called checks. Players buy chips before joining the gaming tables and cash in any that they hold before leaving.

Chips come in five or six different colours, which represent different unit values. The monetary value of a unit can vary in private games, but in casinos and clubs there is a fixed value according to the country in which the game is being played. The unit may be worth, for example, one dollar or one pound.

The values of chips in private games

Chip	Unit value
White	1
Red	5
Blue	10
Yellow	25

The values of chips in casino games

Chip	Unit value
White	1
Red	5
Green	25
Black	100

Chips worth 500 and 1000 units each appear in different colours in different clubs.

It is wise to become familiar with the values of the chips – it is easy to throw down chips in the excitement of the game without realizing just how much money is at stake.

Blackjack

Also called 21, this game is usually for two to six or
seven active players.

In European casinos, other people, known as 'kibitzers',
may 'piggyback' by standing behind an active player,
placing bets on his or her hand.

There can be any number of kibitzers. They may not
advise any player how to play.

The Blackjack table

A regulation table, upon which the game will be played,
is marked with seven places.

The Blackjack table

Other equipment

In addition to the regulation table, the following special equipment is needed:

1 four standard 52-card decks, shuffled together, making one deck of 208 cards;

2 a rack of betting chips;

3 a box for dealing cards, known as the shoe;

4 a box for receiving discards;

5 two jokers, known as 'indicator cards'.

Points value of the cards

Each card has a points value. Ks, Qs and Js count as 10. An ace counts as 1 or 11 at the discretion of the player who holds an ace. The value of a dealer's ace is fixed at 1 or 11 by the house rules and remains constant. In the description of play given here, the dealer's ace is counted as 11.

All other cards (2s to 10s) count at their face value. Because there are four packs of cards in the deck, there will be sixteen of each rank of card, e.g. sixteen aces; four aces of each suit.

Aim

Each player tries to make a higher card count than the dealer, aiming to reach 21 points but going no higher.

Betting limits

Each casino sets its own maximum and minimum limits, which must be announced to the players.

Shuffling and cutting

The dealer shuffles the cards and hands one of the indicator cards to any player, saying 'Cut please.'

The player pushes the indicator card into the deck where he or she wants it cut.

The dealer cuts the deck, putting the indicator card and all the cards in the cut above it underneath the remaining cards, i.e. the indicator is at the bottom of the deck.

The cut

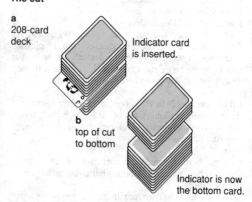

a
208-card deck

Indicator card is inserted.

b
top of cut to bottom

Indicator is now the bottom card.

The second indicator

The dealer places the second indicator card about 50 cards above the bottom one and puts all the cards face down into the dealing shoe.

The top card from the shoe is then discarded.

The cards are now ready for dealing, which will be done after the betting takes place.

The dealing shoe

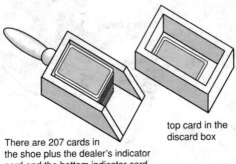

There are 207 cards in
the shoe plus the dealer's indicator
card and the bottom indicator card
which was used for cutting.

top card in the
discard box

Betting
Players bet any amount between the limits by each
placing chips on the betting space directly in front of
them.

A player may bet on several hands, if there are betting
spaces available, but must play to completion the hand
on his or her far right before playing the next hand, and
so on.

Dealing
When betting is complete, the dealer begins with the
player on the left and deals one card face up to
everyone, in clockwise order, and lastly to him- or
herself. The dealer repeats this process, but deals his or
her own second card face down.

The completed deal

dealer's cards

players' cards   direction of
                                                  the deal

Playing

For clarity, each action for play is numbered step by step,
but some steps will be omitted in actual play according
to how the cards come out in the deal.

Step one

Players add up the total value of their two cards.
Any player making a card count of 22 or more is
immediately 'busted' and loses the bet to the banker,
who sweeps it up instantly.
The losing player's two cards are disposed of in the
discard box.

Step two

If the dealer's face-up card is a 10 or an ace, he or she
looks at the face-down card.
If it is a 'natural 21' (two cards totalling 21 exactly) the
dealer places it face up on the table and calls 'blackjack'.
If any other players have a natural 21, they also call and

that hand is declared a stand-off by the dealer. No chips are paid or collected by players who have natural 21s in a stand-off. All other players not having a natural 21 lose to the dealer, who collects their bets.

The natural 21

any ace plus any 10, J, Q or K

Step three
If the dealer does not have a natural 21, play continues, beginning with the player on the dealer's far left.
If the player has a natural 21, he or she says 'blackjack' and the dealer pays that player the winnings. The player's cards are then placed in the discard.

The winning odds
The dealer's odds are fixed at 3 to 2. This means that for every two units the player has bet, he or she wins three units and collects five, i.e. the original stake of two plus the three units won.

Step four
If the two cards dealt to each player do not total 21, each must choose one of two options:
a to stay with the cards dealt because another card might cause a bust by taking the count over 21. The player says 'I stand' and slips the cards under the bet; or

b to draw a card in the hope of improving the count.
The player says 'hit me' or beckons to the dealer who
deals a third card, face up, next to the player's original
pair.

Players may draw as many cards as they like, one at a
time, until they stay by calling 'I stand.'

If the count goes over 21 during the draw, the player
goes bust and loses the bet.

If the count reaches exactly 21, the player
automatically stays.

Step five

The dealer then passes clockwise to the next player,
and so on round the table and back to him- or herself.

The dealer's play

If all the players go bust, the dealer puts his or her own
cards into the discard and starts a new deal.

If some active players remain, the dealer turns both of
his or her cards face up and plays them.

The dealer's options are determined, as follows, by the
rules, marked on the Blackjack table:

1 If the count on two cards is 17 or more, up to 20, the
dealer must stay.

2 If the count is 16 or less, the dealer must draw cards
until the count reaches 17 or more.

The settlement

Beginning with the player on the right and moving anticlockwise around the table, the dealer finally pays off
players who have a higher count than he or she has
with an amount equalling the bet they placed, and
collects the placed bets from players whose count is
lower.

If a player has the same count as the dealer, it is called

a stand-off and neither the player nor the dealer wins or loses; the player keeps the original bet.

Sample of the cards at the end of play

Four active players

player 1

has drawn and stands with a count of 20

player 2

stands with a count of 19

player 3

(opts to score ace as 1)
draws and stands with a count of 20

Sample of the cards at the end of play (continued)
player 4

draws and stands with a count of 16

dealer

has to draw (because the pair counts 14) and stands at 19

The settlements of this sample will be as follows:

player 1:   a win, beating the dealer's count
player 2:   a stand-off, equalling the dealer's count
player 3:   a win, beating the dealer's count
player 4:   a loss, beaten by the dealer's count

As each settlement is made, the dealer scoops up the cards into the discard box.

The next round

In this round, players place their bets again and the dealer makes a new deal from the shoe.

Further shuffling and cutting

When the cards from the shoe have been used up to where the indicator card is, the dealer completes the current deal. After that, all 208 cards are collected together again, the two indicator cards are retrieved and the shuffling and cutting process is repeated before the next deal takes place.

Optional Blackjack rules

In many casinos there are several house rules, the most common of which are insurance betting, splitting pairs and doubling down.

1 Insurance betting. When the dealer's face-up card is an ace, many casinos allow players to make an insurance bet against losing to a possible natural.

In step two, before looking at his or her face-down card, the dealer asks if anyone wants insurance.

Players can insure by adding an amount equal to half their original bet next to their hand.

The dealer then examines his or her face-down card. If it is a 10-count, the pair is a natural, and the dealer turns the card face up. The insurance bettors are paid off at 2 to 1 for every unit they bet.

If the dealer's face-down card is not a 10-count, the insurance bettors lose their insurance bets and the game continues.

2 Splitting pairs. Any two cards of the same rank, regardless of suit, can be treated as a pair. This includes any two cards with a count of 10, such as Q-10 or K-J.

If the original two cards dealt to a player are a pair, the player can split them and have a card dealt on each.

If a dealt card forms another pair, that pair can also be split, and so on.

The player must put the same bet on each of the split hands. He or she must also play those hands, in order, to completion, beginning with the one on the far right.

Three hands made from two pairs

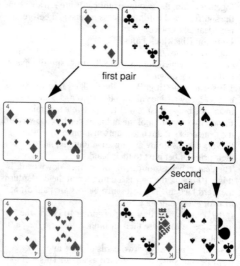

first pair

second pair

If one card of a split pair happens to make a count of 21 with the next card dealt, this does not count as a winning natural and the player is paid off at even money. No player may draw more than one card on any one of two split aces.

3 Doubling down. In some casinos, after the first two cards have been dealt, any player may decide to double the bet and have a third and final card dealt face down onto the original two.

The player may not look at this third card until the dealer turns it face up after the extra stake has been placed and the other players have had their turns.

Chemin de Fer

Chemin de Fer and its cousin Baccarat are French variations of a 15th-century Italian game. Chemin de Fer – often called Shimmy or Chemmy by American gamblers – is currently popular in European casinos; the version called Baccarat is currently more popular in the US. Though similar, Chemin de Fer and Baccarat differ in a few ways – most notably in that the casino takes no risk in Chemin de Fer.

Chemin de Fer means 'railway', a reference to the shoe (card-dealing box) which is passed from player to player as each takes a turn as the dealer.

Unlike in other banking games, when played in casinos the players in Chemin de Fer take turns as banker, playing against each other.

The minimum stake is high and the maximum is often very high.

The casino's role

The casino takes a commission on the banker's winnings, usually five percent. In exchange for this the casino provides the accommodation, the table and the services of two or three croupiers.

The croupiers

Croupiers run the game; the operating croupier supervises the shuffling, cutting and dealing of cards and also takes charge of the bankers' money, collecting their winnings and paying out their losses.

The croupiers also collect the five percent commission on winnings, which is put into the casino's money box, fitted into the centre of the table.

A Chemin de Fer table

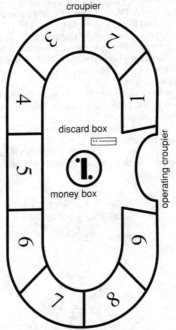

All cards going out of play are dropped into the discard box.

Players at the table

Chemin de Fer is a game for two to as many players as
a table can hold. These players sit round the padded,
green baize table, at numbered places.

In many casinos, some of the players present at the start
of the game may be employees of the casino whose job
it is to encourage play and withdraw when genuine
players come to join the game.

The cards

Eight packs of cards are generally used, though it is
common to find games in which six, three or only one
pack forms the deck.

The cards are dealt from a 'shoe' or sabot, which is a
box made from mahogany.

Each croupier has a long, flat palette with which to
move cards and chips around the table without
stretching.

palette

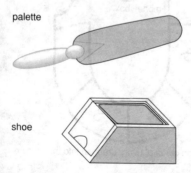

shoe

Points values of the cards

The points values of the cards are as follows:

court cards: 0 points
10s: 0 points
aces: 1 point
2s to 9s: face value

How the points value is totalled

Units of 10 are disregarded. This means that when the total is a one-digit number, that number becomes the points value; if the total is a two-digit number, only the second digit counts, as shown in the examples.

Adding points values

Cards	Total	Points value
	7	7
	13	3
	21	1

Adding points values (continued)

Cards	Total	Points value
5♦ 5♥ Q♦	10	0
A♥ A♦ A♥	3	3
J♠ 5♥ 4♣	9	9
6♣ K♥ 6♦	12	2

Aim

One player, the banker, plays against one other player (known as the active player). Both aim to get a score of 9 or the closest to it. The one with the higher score wins.

If the players make the same count, new cards are dealt and nobody collects or loses.

Shuffling and cutting the cards

The following routine is followed whenever the whole deck is to be shuffled.

1 The operating croupier spreads all eight packs of cards face up on the table. It is usual to use four packs with red backs and four with blue, preferably all of the same pattern.

2 All the players and croupiers take piles of the cards and shuffle them, until all the cards have been shuffled.

3 The croupier takes the shuffled cards from each player. After shuffling them together, the croupier places them in little piles, usually seven or eight.

4 The croupier invites the players to cut as many of the piles as they wish, without exposing any card.

5 Players who want to make a cut do so one at a time beginning with the player to the croupier's right.

6 The croupier cuts any of the cards as he or she chooses.

7 Finally the croupier stacks all the cards into the shoe ready for play.

The first banker

The player sitting immediately to the right of the croupier has the option of being the first banker. If he or she doesn't want the bank, it passes to the next player anticlockwise, who may keep it or pass it on.

In some casinos there is an auction for the bank, which
goes to the highest bidder. The casino collects the
auction bid.

Betting

The croupier slides the shoe to the first banker who
places a bet (of any amount between the house limits)
on the area of the table known as the piste.

The croupier handles the banker's chips.

The banker then slides the top three cards out of the
shoe and hands them to the croupier, who drops them
into the discard box.

Fading

The stake placed by the banker can be equalled, but not
exceeded, by bets from the other players. The process
of betting is known as 'fading the bank'.

Anyone wanting to fade the bank completely, i.e. stake
the same as the bank, places the bet on the piste and
calls 'banco'.

If more than one player calls banco, the one sitting
nearest to the right side of the banker takes precedence.
This player is then known as the ponte and becomes the
active player.

If nobody calls banco, players may, in anticlockwise
order from the banker's right, place partial bets until the
bank is completely faded. The total bets cannot exceed
the banker's bet as he or she cannot pay out more than
the amount staked if the bet is lost.

If the bank is not faded completely, the excess is set
aside from the banker's bet, for the banker.

A bet placed on the line of the piste is worth only half
its normal value and is known as a 'cheval'.

When there is no ponte, the player making the highest
bet becomes the active player.

When a player calls 'banco'

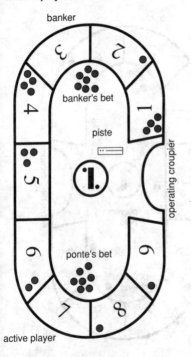

When a player bets a cheval

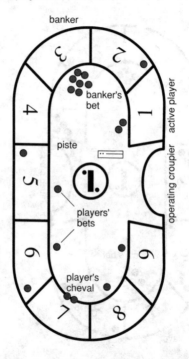

Dealing

Bankers deal by sliding one card out of the shoe and dealing it face down to the active player. They then deal one card face down to themselves, another to the active player and finally another to themselves.

Playing the first round

In this round, the active player looks at his or her dealt cards.

Situation 1. If a player's cards total 8 or 9 points, the player puts them face up on the table and the banker must show his or her cards.

Whoever has the higher score wins.

If the banker wins, the croupier collects all the bets from all the players and gives them to the banker.

If the active player wins, the croupier pays, from the banker's bet, all the players an amount equal to their original bet.

Situation 2. If at any time the active player and the banker have the same points count, their cards are discarded and the banker makes a new deal.

Situation 3. If the active player's cards total less than 8, the player calls 'pass'.

The banker then examines his or her own cards. If they total 8 or 9, the banker wins. The cards are turned face up and the banker collects the bets.

If they total less than 8, the banker calls 'pass' and the second round begins with the active player's turn again.

Playing the second and final round

In this round, the active player must draw or stay according to his or her count.

Situation 4. If the active player's count is 6 or 7, the player must stay.

Rules for the banker's second turn

Bankers must draw or stay according to these rules, unless they have an option, marked d/s, allowing them to choose whether to draw or stay.

Banker's count:	3	4	5	6	7
Value of active player's draw					
0	draw	stay	stay	stay	stay
1	draw	stay	stay	stay	stay
2	draw	draw	stay	stay	stay
3	draw	draw	stay	stay	stay
4	draw	draw	d/s	stay	stay
5	draw	draw	draw	stay	stay
6	draw	draw	draw	draw	stay
7	draw	draw	draw	draw	stay
8	stay	stay	stay	stay	stay
9	d/s	stay	stay	stay	stay

If the count is 5, the player has the option to stay or draw.

If the player stays, the banker must then act according to the following rules:

a if the banker's count is 6 or 7, he or she must stay;

b if the banker's count is 5 or less, he or she must draw a card from the top of the deck in the shoe.

The winner is then the one with the higher score and collects as before.

Situation 5. If the active player's count is 0, 1, 2, 3 or 4, he or she must draw a card. If it is 5, the player may choose to draw rather than stay.

The drawn card is placed face up on the table, and the banker must respond according to the table shown opposite. The banker's response depends on the count the banker holds and the value of the active player's draw card.

After the second turn is complete, whoever has the higher count wins and collects as before. A tie always invalidates the counts: the cards are discarded and a new deal takes place without any further betting.

Continuing play

Play continues in this fashion. The banker may pass the shoe of cards on to the right-hand neighbour whenever there are no bets on the table.

When the deck of cards runs out, the croupier opens new packs, which are shuffled and cut as before.

Chinese Fan Tan

This game was originally played with dice, but cards are now often used to determine the count, as described here. The game is a total gamble; no skill is involved. Although not played in public clubs (presumably because the banker has no advantage), private games at home are popular.

The original card version of Fan Tan, however, is neither a banking game nor a complete gamble. Fan Tan requires considerable skill and is a very simple and enjoyable social or family game. (See Section 3 for a full description of Fan Tan.)

Players

Any number of players can play against the banker. The banker can be chosen by draw, and the position rotates after an agreed number of games so that everyone has a turn.

Cards and chips

In Chinese Fan Tan, a standard deck of 52 cards is used, plus one joker which is placed face up on the table.

Players are given an equal number of chips with which to bet. If possible, each player should have a different colour or type of chip.

The four corners of the joker are designated 1, 2, 3 and 4, from the bottom left corner, clockwise.

Betting

The house limits how much can be bet and how many bets each player can place. Within these limits, players bet by placing chips on one or more of the four numbers.

A chip placed at the corner of the joker indicates a bet on only that number.

A chip placed along the side of the joker indicates a bet on the two numbers on either nearby corner.

Players can place as many bets as they like and stake as many chips as they like on each bet. More than one player can make the same bet.

Example of bets in place

banker

A is a bet that number 3 will win.
B is a bet that 1 or 4 will win.
C is a bet that 2 or 1 will win.

Aim

Players gamble on which of the four numbers will win.
Only one number wins.

Shuffling and counting

Any player shuffles the cards and places them face
down on the table.

The banker then cuts from the deck a large packet of
cards (at least one-third of the deck) and counts them,
four at a time. If the packet can be counted out exactly
in fours, the winning number is 4. Otherwise the
remaining number of cards is the winning number.

Sample counts

Packet size	Winning number
37	1
31	3
21	1
22	2
23	3
24	4

The payoff

When the winning number has been revealed, the
banker pays bets on a single number at odds of 3 to 1.
Bets on two numbers are paid even money if one of the
pair wins.

The bank collects all bets on non-winning numbers.

Faro

This game probably originated in Italy. In its early days
at the French court it was called Pharaon because one
of the Ks in the old French deck of cards looked like an
Egyptian Pharaoh.

Faro became popular in America in the 19th century,
when fortunes were won and lost on the riverboats of
New Orleans, in the gambling dens of Washington and
the saloons of the West.

In the western states of the US, a sign of a tiger hanging
outside a gambling house indicated that Faro was
played there. Hence the nickname Bucking the Tiger.

Equipment

The game requires the following special equipment:

1 A rectangular table covered with green felt. Painted
on it are the thirteen cards of a suit, usually spades, and
space for a particular kind of bet known as High Card.

2 A standard 52-card deck. The rank order of the cards is from ace (low) to K (high). Only the rank order counts; suits are not significant.

Rank

low

high

The top of a Faro table

High Card

3 A special Faro dealing box from which the cards are
dealt. It was designed to prevent cheating.

Features of a Faro dealing box

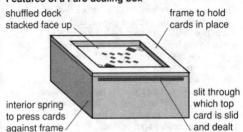

shuffled deck
stacked face up

frame to hold
cards in place

interior spring
to press cards
against frame

slit through
which top
card is slid
and dealt

4 A rack of house chips kept to the right of the dealer.
5 Betting chips, bought by the players. Each player is
given a different colour of chip to avoid confusion
when betting.

The unit value of chips depends on the country and the
casino in which the game is played; each chip could be
worth two dollars or one pound, for example.

6 Markers to indicate that a bet has been placed that is
equal in value to the one a player has already placed
elsewhere on the table.

Markers are flat, white rectangles, usually made of
plastic, used when a player has run out of chips.

7 Faro coppers for betting that a certain card will lose.
Originally copper pennies, modern Faro coppers are flat
plastic hexagonals in red or black. They are sometimes
placed on top of the markers or chips.

Chips, markers and coppers

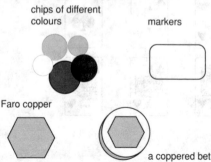

chips of different
colours

markers

Faro copper

a coppered bet

8 A counting rack known as the casekeeper. It allows a record to be kept of exactly which cards have been played and whether they won or lost. This is visible to all players at all times.

Features of a Faro casekeeper

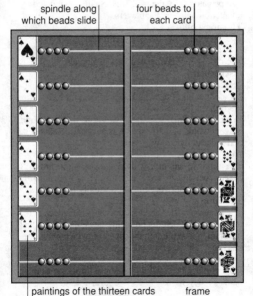

spindle along which beads slide

four beads to each card

paintings of the thirteen cards of a suit, usually spades

frame

Players

Any number of people can play Faro. The table can usually comfortably seat ten players plus three house-players who are casino employees: the dealer, the casekeeper and the lookout. The players play against the bank, i.e. the casino.

In a private game, the banker is usually designated by an auction between the players.

The house-players

The dealer handles the cards, chips and markers and runs the game.

The casekeeper is operated by a person also known as a casekeeper.

The lookout supervises the markers and the payment and collection of bets while seated on a high chair to the right of the dealer.

In a private game, the banker would be the dealer and players would usually take turns at being casekeeper and lookout by a draw.

Aim

The aim is to win money by making bets on cards. Players bet on cards to win or lose. This is a game of pure chance with very little opportunity for skill.

Shuffling

The dealer shuffles and cuts the cards. The deck is then placed into the dealing box with the cards face up and the frame closed. Later, the top card, which everyone has seen, will be removed.

Betting

Players place bets, within the house limits, on as many cards as they wish.

How the chips are used to make bets

A player can bet on one card or on more than one card, and places chips accordingly. This is done as shown in the sample table on the following pages. If a player bets on more than one card and loses on one of the cards, he or she loses the bet completely, but may bet again on one or more of them, as desired.

The payment of winnings or losses

Two cards from the deck are drawn at each turn: the one drawn out first is called the loser card, and the second is the winner card.

Payment or collection is made only on these two cards at each draw. The payment is evens.

Sample winnings and losses

If three chips are placed on a card to be the winner and that card is drawn a winner, then the player collects both his or her bet and a further three chips from the bank.

If the card on which the player bet is the loser card, the bank collects the bet.

If the card on which the player bet is neither the winner nor the loser, the bet stays in place until that card is drawn at a later turn.

Similarly, if a player bets on a card to be a loser and it is the first card drawn from the pack, he or she wins the bet. If it is the winner card, the player loses the bet.

Dealing and playing a turn

After the bets have been laid, the dealer removes the top, visible card, known as the 'soda', from the dealing box and places it next to his or her chip rack to form the winning discards or 'soda stack'.

Sample bets on a Faro table

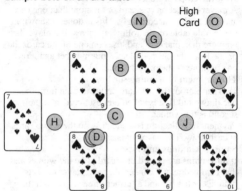

Key to sample bets

A Bet on one card, e.g. the 4.

B Bet on two neighbouring cards, e.g. 6 and 5. When betting 6 and 7 or 7 and 8, the chip is placed between the two adjacent corners of the cards.

C Bet on two diagonal cards, e.g. 6 and 9, when betting only one chip. If a player bets one card to win and the other to lose, he or she puts a copper on the to-lose card and tilts the chip (placed on top of the copper) toward the card to win.

D Bet on two diagonal cards, e.g. 5 and 8, when betting more than one chip. This bet cannot be used on

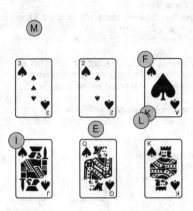

a 7. Known as a 'heeled bet', the top chips are tilted toward the other card being bet on. Players copper the top chip only if they bet both to lose.

E Bet on neighbouring cards, e.g. 2 and Q.

F Bet on one card and its next-but-one neighbour, e.g. ace and 3, jumping the 2. It cannot be placed where there is no neighbour to jump over: i.e. on the 7, the left side of the 5, 6, 8 or 9, or the right side of the ace, 2, Q or K.

G Bet on three neighbouring cards, e.g. 4, 5 and 6. This bet cannot be used on the ace, K or 7.

H Bet on 6, 7 and 8 only.

I Bet on three neighbouring cards, one horizontal and one vertical, e.g. 3, J and 10.

J Bet on four cards forming a square, e.g. 4, 5, 9 and 10.

K and **L** Same bets as **C** and **D**, but the ace is bet to lose and the Q to win. The copper is placed on **K**.

M Bet that the winner/loser card will be an even number.

N Bet that the winner/loser card will be an odd number.

O Bet that the winner card will be a higher rank than the loser card.

Example of the table at the first turn

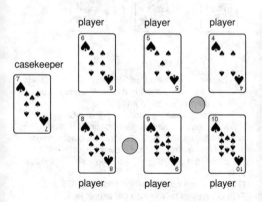

The next card (the loser card) is removed and placed by
the dealing box to start the loser stack.

The second card (the winner card) remains exposed in
the dealing box.

Winnings and losses are collected and paid as appropriate to each player.

Any bets on cards that have not appeared remain in
place for the next turn.

Casekeeping

The casekeeper records which cards have been drawn.
As a card is played, a bead on the appropriate row of
the casekeeper is moved. For example, if an 8 is drawn
as the winning card, one of the four beads on the 8s row

Sample of part of the casekeeper in action

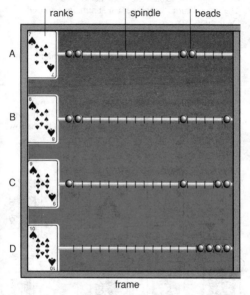

Key

A two 7s in deck; two 7s drawn as winners

B two 8s in deck; two drawn, one winner, one loser

C one 9 in deck; three drawn, one winner, two losers

D no 10s in deck; all drawn and out of play

is moved along the spindle until it is about an inch from
the frame.

If the 8 is the loser card, the bead is moved to touch the
frame.

When all four cards of the same rank have been drawn,
all four beads are pushed together at the end of the
spindle, indicating that there are no more of that rank in
the deck.

The next and subsequent turns

The dealer invites players to lay bets as they wish.
Players may, in between turns, also change any of their
bets that remain on the table.

The dealer removes the top card from the dealing box
(the winner card from the last turn) which now
becomes the soda and is also placed on the soda stack.

The turn begins when the next card is drawn and placed
on the loser pile beside the dealing box. This is now the
loser card for this turn.

The winner card is the one remaining in the box.

Winnings and losses are collected and paid as before.

The next deal

Play continues in this way until all cards have been
dealt but one. This last is called the hock card and does
not make or lose bets. It is placed onto the soda stack.

All the cards are then shuffled and cut again by the
dealer, and play continues as before.

The last turn

This occurs when the casekeeper shows that there are
only three cards left in the dealing box. Everyone
knows what those three cards must be.

This stage is called the last turn and the player who is
active at the time has a choice on how to bet.

The player can either bet on one or more of the
remaining cards as usual or may decide to 'call the turn',
i.e. bet that he or she can call the order in which the last
three will be drawn.

An example of calling the last turn
If the last three cards are the 2 of spades, 8 of hearts and
K of diamonds, a player calling the turn might place a
bet on 8 of hearts to lose and K of diamonds to win.
The player would then call the cards as follows:

first card, to lose: 8 of hearts
second card, to win: K of diamonds
third card, the hock: 2 of spades

The player calls the last turn by placing the bet on that
edge or corner of the loser card facing the to-win card.
To call the last turn with more than one chip, the top chip
is tilted on top of the bottom chip toward the to-win card.
To call with only one chip, the player must place a
copper on the edge of the card, then place a chip on the
copper and tilt the chip. The chip is then covered by
another copper to make clear that the player is calling the
turn and not simply heeling a bet.

Players wishing to call a last turn on two cards separated
on the table by a third must tilt their bets toward the
outside edge of the table, thereby indicating their wish to
go round the middle card.

The payoff on the last turn
If the call is correct, the payoff is 4 to 1. If not, the caller
loses the bet.

If there are two cards of the same rank left in the box,
then the payoff is only 2 to 1. This is called a 'cat-hop'.

If the last three cards are all the same rank, but include
red and black – for example, two red Js and one black J,

the player calls the order in which the colours will
appear. The payoff is the same as a cat-hop.

If a player bet on one or more of the remaining cards in
the usual way, then the bets are paid and collected in the
usual way. However, if a player has bet on the hock card
then the result is a stand-off.

Mistakes in casekeeping or dealing

If mistakes have not been seen and corrected by the
lookout and at the last turn the casekeeper does not show
three cards remaining in the box, then the dealer checks
through the winning and losing discard piles to correct
the error on the casekeeper.

If the dealer has made the mistake and the last turn
shows only two cards, not three, then the last turn is void.

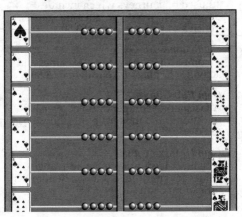

COLLINS GEM

Other Gem titles that may interest you include:

Gem Card Games
A handy guide that explains the rules and strategies of play for a wide variety of popular family card games **£3.50**

Gem Travel Games
An indispensable help in keeping children amused on journeys which includes observation, word and guessing games, and pencil and paper games **£3.50**

Gem Games for One
A compact guide to over 100 games and activities to play on your own **£3.50**

Gem Pub Games
A fascinating compendium of over 100 traditional and modern public house pastime **£3.50**

Gem Holiday Games
A handy-sized guide to a wide range of games for children to play on holiday with little or no equipment **£3.50**